RESEARCH REPORT NO. 130

GLOBALIZATION AND
THE SOUTHERN AFRICAN ECONOMIES

Edited by
Mats Lundahl

Nordiska Afrikainstitutet, Uppsala 2004

Indexing terms
Southern Africa
Globalization
International Economy
Trade
Economics
Economic development
Economic reform
Labour market

Language checking: Elaine Almén

ISSN 1104-8425

ISBN 91-7106-532-6

© the authors and Nordiska Afrikainstitutet, 2004

Printed in Sweden by Elanders Infologistics Väst AB, 2004

Contents

Preface

In the mid-1990s the Swedish Council for Planning and Coordination of Research (Forskningsrådsnämnden – FRN) – subsequently merged into the Council of Science (Vetenskaprådet) – established a national, interdisciplinary research committee on Global Processes. The Committee has been strongly committed to a multidimensional and multidisciplinary approach to globalization and global processes and to using regional perspectives. Several collective studies have come out of its work: *Globalizations and Modernities. Experiences and Perspectives of Europe and Latin America* (1999), *Globalization and Its Impact on Chinese and Swedish Society* (2000), *The New Federalism* (2000), all published by FRN in Stockholm (in English), and *Globalizations Are Plural*, a special issue of *International Sociology* (Vol. 15, No. 2, 2000). Selected papers from the conference on Asia and Europe in Global Processes, held in Singapore in March 2001, will appear in Göran Therborn and Habibul Haque Khondkar (eds.), *Asia and Europe in Globalization: Continents, Regions and Nations*, published by E.J. Brill, Leiden. The present volume completes the regional perspective.

The chapters in this report derive from a conference at the iKhaya Guest Lodge and Conference Centre in Cape Town, 29 November–2 December 2001, organized together with the University of Cape Town. The report covers one of the three broad themes: economic issues. A companion volume, also published by the Nordic Africa Institute, deals with family and gender issues (African Families in a Global Context, edited by Göran Therborn).

As conference participant I very much enjoyed the encounters of different disciplinary perspectives and of different continental, regional and national experiences. I hope that the readers as well will find some pleasure in the variety of vistas, as well as in the individual contributions.

The editing was finished during my residence at the Swedish Collegium for Advanced Study in the Social Sciences (SCASSS) at Uppsala University. This support is gratefully acknowledged.

Uppsala, 22 December 2003

Mats Lundahl

Author Presentations

Arne Bigsten is Professor of Development Economics at the School of Economics and Commercial Law at Göteborg University. He has published extensively on development issues with particular emphasis on income distribution, poverty and growth. The geographical focus has mainly been on Africa.

Michael Bratton is Professor of Political Science and African Studies at Michigan State University. With Robert Mattes and E. Gyimah Boadi, he is the co-founder ad co-director of the Afrobarometer, a comparative series of national public opinion surveys in fifteen African countries. Their forthcoming book *Learning about Reform: People, Democracy and Markets in Africa* will be published in 2004.

Dick Durevall is Senior Lecturer at the Department of Economics, School of Economics and Commercial Law, Göteborg University, and at the Department of Economic and Social Sciences, the University of Skövde. He has undertaken research on macroeconomics and the international trade of developing countries, and published articles on Brazil, Kenya, Malawi and Zimbabwe. He is at present researching the impact of globalization in Sub-Saharan Africa.

Mats Lundahl is Professor of Development Economics at the Stockholm School of Economics. His major research fields are economic development, international economics and historical economics. His work on Africa has dealt mainly with South Africa, Lesotho and Tanzania.

Robert Mattes is Associate Professor of Political Studies and Director of the Democracy in Africa Research Unit in the Centre for Social Studies at the University of Cape Town. He is also an Associate with the Institute for Democracy in South Africa (Idasa). His research has focused on the development of a democratic political culture in South Africa and across the continent and on the impact of race and identity in voting behaviour and attitude formation in South Africa.

Lennart Petersson is Associate Professor of Economics, School of Economics and Management, Lund University, Sweden. His research is directed towards international trade and regional integration and location of industry in southern Africa.

Natalie Pienaar has a degree in economics from the University of the Witwatersrand, South Africa. She is currently completing her PhD at the Institute for International Economic Studies at Stockholm University. Her main field of interest is trade policy, with particular emphasis on World Trade Organization (WTO) agreements.

Edward Webster is Professor of Sociology and Director of the Sociology of Work Unit (SWOP) at the University of the Witwatersrand. He has directed international research projects for such organizations as the ILO (International Labour Organization), UNRISD (United Nations Research Institute for Social Development), the UK Department for International Development (DFID) and the MacArthur Foundation in Chicago. His PhD thesis was on the changing employment patterns and skills in foundries in the metal industry in South Africa.

1. Introduction: Africa in Global Context

Mats Lundahl

Globalization is a buzzword that is being used under all conceivable circumstances. We are living in an 'era of globalization', where the four corners of the world have come together, where commodity and factor markets are strongly interlinked, where technologies spread from more advanced to less advanced regions, where information travels virtually instantaneously, where financial capital moves in milliseconds, where economic policies in different countries tend to be more and more entangled with each other, where political systems spread, mainly from the western democracies to other parts of the world, where different cultures borrow elements from each other and fuse them, where legal systems clash and influence one another, where traditional family and gender patterns are broken up as a result of foreign influences, where religions confront each other etc. There is virtually no end to the list, and it is difficult to resist global influences. True, there is a growing movement against the liberal forms of globalization, the so-called Porto Alegre current, but this movement is increasingly seeing its fight as one for alternative global processes. Even the dark side of globalization, international terrorism, rides the crest of the wave and makes use of the technologies that have contributed to shrinking the world. The tide is irresistible, and whatever ideological views you hold, it cannot be met in an ostrich-like fashion, but you must tackle the problems it creates (and make use of the promises it makes) in a head-on conscious fashion.

The actors in this globalized setting are as many as the forms that globalization assumes: firms, workers, farmers, international organizations like the World Bank, the International Monetary Fund, the World Trade Organization, and the many different specialized agencies of the United Nations system, international non-governmental organizations, churches, consumers of information spread via more or less global mass media, music listeners, art viewers, book readers, internet users … Again, there is no end to their number.

A problem with this variety of forms and actors is that it is not at all clear what globalization means, or rather, it means very different things to different people. It all depends on the particular setting and circumstances. Globalization is not globalization, but globalizations, and globalizations are plural, not singular. They are economic, cultural, social, cognitive, normative, political; you name them. Once again, the diversity is overwhelming.

A second problem with the globalization concept is that very frequently, globalization is implicitly thought of as a state: the current state of the world at the beginning of the twenty-first century. This, however, is a misconception. Globalization is not a state; it is a process. It is the process that created the globalized world, and this process cannot be understood, except in a historical perspective. We need to come to grips with the very mechanisms that brought us to where we are today. In the present work we will define globalization, or globalizations (the two terms will be used interchangeably) as the processes creating tendencies to a world-wide reach, impact and connectedness of social phenomena in a wide sense and a world-encompassing awareness among social actors.

Globalization in History

With this perspective it is possible to identify a number of major globalization waves or episodes across the history of mankind. The first consisted of the diffusion of world religions and the establishment of civilizations covering major parts of the continents. The main period extended from the fourth to the eighth centuries AD. This was the period when Christianity gained a strong foothold in the European continent and established outposts in Africa and India. Simultaneously, the other world religions, Hinduism, Buddhism and Islam, expanded out of their core areas, across continents and from one continent to another. Confucianism spread across China and neighbouring territories. All these religions had their own, unifying, holy languages and were carriers of specific cultures.

The second wave of globalization consisted of the creation of the most wide-ranging continuous empire that the world has ever seen – up to the present day: the Mongol empire. Out of incredibly small and volatile beginnings, a people consisting of perhaps a million souls at the beginning of the thirteenth century managed to wreak major havoc on all the major civilizations surrounding it and govern a territory that extended from Eastern Europe to the Sea of Japan, and from the Indo-Chinese border and the Persian Gulf to southern Siberia and the northern parts of European Russia. For the first time in history Europe acquired a reliable knowledge about China and the Orient. Two continents were brought closer together. The Mongol episode also served to solidify some of the long-distance trade network that had been established from about 1000 to around 1350, linking the British Isles in the west with China and Indonesia, and with parts of Africa south of the Sahara.

Shortly after the fall of the Mongol Yuan dynasty in China, the Chinese undertook a series of major voyages that brought them to the east coast of Africa, and had it not been for a sudden inward turn in imperial policy they might well have discovered the sea route to Europe. Instead, the protagonist role in the third wave of globalization, that of the geographical discoveries and territorial conquests, fell to the Europeans, notably the two Iberian kingdoms of Portugal and Spain during the fifteenth and sixteenth centuries, and the Dutch, British and French thereafter, up to around 1750. Asia was linked closer to Europe, and the Americas made their entry in the global arena. Subsequently, European wars were fought not only on the European continent but on the lands and in the waters of overseas territories as well. War had acquired a global character.

At this point, a major break with the past took place in world history: the industrial revolution. This first led to increased globalization of commerce, via the triangular trade pattern that saw European manufactures flow to North America and Africa, African slaves supplying the American plantations, and North American raw materials going into the industrial production of Europe. The industrial revolution also constituted the prerequisite for the fourth major globalization episode: the gradual diffusion of the new technology across the European continent, eastwards to Russia, and to post-Meiji Japan, as well as the creation of the 'north-south' type of trade pattern that was to culminate in the golden age of transport revolution, commodity trade, labor migration and capital movements from about 1870 to the outbreak of World War I. During this period European manufactures were regularly exchanged for primary products from the regions of recent settlement and less developed regions elsewhere in America, Africa and Asia. China and Japan were opened up by force to international trade. This period also saw the culmination of the territorial competition between the major European colonial powers, with the division of Africa. The First World War and the Great Depression provided the end point of this globalization wave, and a retreat from global patterns.

The fifth wave of globalization began with World War II, which was a great deal more global than World War I, involving major war theatres not only in Europe but in North Africa, Africa east of India and the Pacific as well. One of the major results of the war was the gradual dissolution of the colonial empires, with the exception of the Soviet Union. Another was the regrouping of the major powers that resulted in the Cold War, involving all parts of planet earth.

The collapse of the Soviet Union may perhaps be put as the symbolic starting point of the sixth, hitherto unfinished, globalization episode, but some of the major mechanisms had evolved gradually during the late 1970s and the 1980s. International trade expanded, capital movements were increasingly freed of obstacles, the European and North Atlantic economies were linked closer to one another, not only in terms of commodity and factor movements, spread of technology and transnationalization of firms, but also in terms of policy interdependence, mainly economically, but to an increasing extent also politically. The former communist states have been drawn into the western orbit. The internationalization of the means of telecommunication and the mass media has been little short of revolutionary. All these tendencies have grown stronger on the one hand, and have spread across an ever vaster geographic territory on the other.

The Place of Africa

The present volume deals with Africa and the place of the African continent and states in global economic processes. Africa does not figure prominently in any of the globalization waves or episodes that we have just summarized. It was touched by the early spread of the world religions, but only marginally. The repercussions in Africa of the shock that the Mongols subjected Asia and Europe to were comparatively minor. The geographical discoveries at first deliberately bypassed Africa, notably the interior of the continent. The slave trade and the later exchange of manufactures for primary products were limited to coastal areas as well, and the territorial division of the continent among the colonial powers constitutes the last act in the drama of western European imperialist expansion. The post World War II period in a sense marked a retreat of Africa from global processes as the political and economic ties with the European powers were severed, and in the surge of globalization that has taken place during the last few decades, Africa has been increasingly marginalized.

The marginal position of Africa does, however, not mean that a study of the continent from the point of view of globalization and global processes is unwarranted. Globalization has definitely had an impact on Africa, and the purpose of the present volume is to contribute to the understanding of how global processes are interpreted in and affect Africa, but not only that. Africa has also made contributions to global processes, and in that sense it would be wrong to view the continent as the child of sorrow of contemporary modernity. Africa should be analyzed not only as a recipient or a victim but also in its role as an active contributor, without letting any ideological, diplomatic or politically correct blinkers limit the view.

The idea of the present volume is somewhat more limited: to find out how global trade and investment patterns affect African societies, how workplace relations are affected by global economic processes and by discourses and demands for change voiced, for example, via the UN system and the apparatus of international development cooperation as a whole.

Economic Issues

Three main issues call for attention. The first has to do with Africa's position in the world economy and the relations with its main actors, and how this position has changed over time. The second is the identification of the overall economic trends in the African continent. Finally, the various responses to globalization call for analysis. For a long time Africa has been on the periphery of international economic currents. At present we are witnessing a strong trend towards increasing interdependence in world trade, investment and transfer of technology as well as in terms of economic policies. An increasing number of countries in the third world are moving away from import substitution in the direction of outward-oriented policies. Many African nations have, however, been slow in making the adjustments or have failed to do so at all. Has Africa been left behind or can it become an important part of the global economic context?

With globalization also comes the need for greater economic integration. A number of regional cooperation efforts are currently in operation in Africa, e.g. the Southern African Customs Union (SACU), the Southern African Development Community (SADC) and the Common Market for Eastern and Southern Africa (COMESA). Efforts like these of course have implications both for political and economic stability within Africa and for the continent's relations with the rest of the world. Lastly, when faced with the current wave of globalization the African nations have had to think of appropriate responses, normally how to facilitate participation and at the same time minimize the potential damage to vulnerable groups. Governments have to think of the implications of globalization in terms of the degree of freedom with which they can act in matters of both international and domestic policy.

Chapter 2, by Mats Lundahl and Natalie Pienaar, focuses on the place of Africa in the global economy. They provide an account of the expansion of international trade and foreign direct investment during the 1980s and 1990s and compare the general trends with those prevailing in Africa. The result is unequivocal: Africa is lagging sadly behind. The continent was in an economic crisis during both decades and it lost terrain both in terms of its share of world trade and as a recipient of investment. The main reasons behind the deterioration have been subject to considerable debate. However, the bulk of the evidence seems to indicate that it was domestic rather than external factors that were responsible. Export, import and exchange rate policies militated against participation and other policies served to destroy markets or at least hamper their functioning. Reform attempts have frequently been blocked by domestic politics, a number of reforms actually undertaken have been half-hearted and undermined by deficient state apparatuses and outright corruption. Even in countries where reforms were carried out more or less 'by the book' growth rates have not increased to the extent expected. Whether Africa will break out of the impasse remains to be seen. There are many obstacles to be overcome, excessive centralization, deficient education, HIV/AIDS, faulty economic policies and corruption, to mention but a few. The challenge continues to be there.

Africa has failed to defend its position in the world economy during the present wave of globalization, but is it necessarily true that globalization is good for Africa? This question is posed in Chapter 3, by Arne Bigsten and Dick Durevall. They begin by examining the African growth record and the constraints to growth in rural and urban areas, and conclude that growth has been hampered by a combination of poor institutions and bad policies. After a discussion of the relationship between trade and growth in the African case, they then turn to a more detailed examination of the political economy of adjustment in Africa and conclude that basically the African crisis is a crisis of governance. The redistributive nature of the state and its connection with ethnic and political conflicts plays an important role, and there are no forces in Africa which can guarantee good governance. Democratic control is weak. Hence ineffective policies persist, and reforms are implemented in a biased fashion. For successful integration into the world economy a liberalization of the flows of goods is required, since this reduces the scope for rent-seeking via arbitrage between international and domestic prices, but in practice policies often work in the opposite direction, because they are designed to favour certain groups. In the final section, Bigsten and Durevall use the recent example of Zimbabwe to provide a concrete illustration of their argument. Integration into the global economy is no panacea, but it does at least reduce the scope for corrupt, unproductive policies.

One of the main components of globalization in Africa is economic reform. This frequently takes on the shape imposed by the international financial institutions, i.e. the World Bank and the IMF. The typical structural adjustment program entails the scrapping of quantitative import restrictions, the lowering and unification of tariff levels, devaluation of the currency, abolition of price controls and parastatal marketing organizations, liberalization of capital movements, etc. The idea is to get away from inefficient production structures and to concentrate resources in the branches that have a comparative advantage, and hence increase the growth rate of the economy. This so-called Washington consensus has met with considerable resistance in some instances. Critics have argued that the programs impose too heavy costs on the economy, notably on poor and vulnerable groups.

In Chapter 4, Michael Bratton and Robert Mattes analyze the popular reaction to economic reform programs in southern Africa. A series of interviews were carried out in seven countries, Botswana, Lesotho, Malawi, Namibia, Zambia, Zimbabwe and South Africa, in order to find out what people in general knew about the contents of the reform programs and what their attitudes to them and the general economic conditions prevailing were. As might perhaps be expected, attitudes varied, and the picture that emerges is not altogether consistent. While many of the fundamental values underlying the reform efforts were espoused by the respondents, at the same time people manifested a strong desire that the state take responsibility for employment and provision of basic economic services. Market pricing was seen as positive in so far as it contributed to an increased supply of goods, but there was considerable doubt whether the market forces would lead to increased employment and higher incomes. The responses were conditioned by the socio-economic background of the respondents. Especially the poor were suspicious of the ability of structural adjustment to improve conditions. The upwardly-mobile, better educated population segments, on the other hand, tended to regard the reforms as an opportunity instead of as a threat.

One of the features of the present wave of globalization is the tendency for states to enter into economic agreements with other states: free trade areas, customs unions, common markets, etc. Strictly speaking, economic integration has two sides. From the point of view of the non-participants this represents a retreat from globalization, but from the point of view of the integrating nations it facilitates the flows of goods, factors and technologies. This trend has not passed Africa by. In Chapter 5, Mats Lundahl and Lennart Petersson examine the extent to which southern Africa may be thought of as an economic region. During the 1990s, the economies of Africa south of the Sahara underwent an opening up and liberalization process, with tariff reduction and exchange rate adjustment as the main ingredients. At the same time a number of regional integration efforts were initiated, reformed or strengthened, ranging from free trade initiatives almost to economic unions.

The fourteen SADC countries in the region differ substantially with respect to their economic characteristics, and all of them do not participate in each and every effort. The oldest institution is also the most far-reaching one: the Southern African Customs Union (SACU), consisting of South Africa, Botswana, Lesotho, Namibia and Swaziland, which comes close to being a common market and which entails a great deal of policy coordination as well. All the SACU members, except Botswana, also form part of the Common Monetary Area (CMA). Eight countries collaborate in the Regional Integration Facilitation Forum (RIFF), an attempt to harmonize tariff levels. Eighteen sub-Saharan countries combine with Egypt, Djibouti and the Sudan in the not too successful Common Market for Eastern and Southern Africa (COMESA) which has on its agenda the unrealistic goal of the establishment of a customs union by 2004. The Southern African Development Community (SADC) works for cooperation between the southern African states in most sectors of the economy, and the SADC Free Trade Area, which encompasses eleven of the fourteen SADC members, is at work on the removal of obstacles to free trade in the area. The extent of coordination between the different arrangements is, however, low. There is not only partial overlapping but partial inconsistency as well.

The prospects for increased trade in the region are uneven. The main problem is the dominance of South Africa, a country which has its main suppliers overseas. So far this has made it difficult for the other countries in the region to develop exports for the South African market, especially non-traditional exports. As far as macroeconomic stability is concerned the experience differs widely, with Mauritius and the SACU countries doing relatively well, while the non-SACU economies have been dependent on foreign aid for stability. As a whole, Lundahl and Petersson conclude that the regional integration effort in southern Africa has not produced the desired results. The discrepancies in terms of living standards and economic structures have also made for differences in terms of benefits. Yet, the effort continues.

Chapter 6, by Edward Webster, shifts the focus to the local South African arena. The issue is the influence of globalization on the world of work and labor in southern Africa in general (Zambia, Botswana, Zimbabwe and Mozambique) and in particular the role of South Africa in the region. In order to understand the impact, globalization has to be grounded in the institutional realities of southern Africa, not least the legacy of the white settlers: export orientation, labor migration and land alienation, and in the case of South Africa, the apartheid workplace regime. The economic liberalization that has taken place in southern Africa has led both to connection and disconnection. The former process has worked through the formation of regional trading blocks, the intensification of communication, the increased variety of consumer goods, the spread of values of democracy and human rights, the introduction of new workplace norms, modern management and privatization of state assets. This draws new people into the regional elites. Disconnection in turn has to do with the loss of formal jobs and the increasing role of the informal sector in survival strategies, and this, Webster argues, affects the majority in southern Africa.

The changing nature of work in the southern African region calls for new responses to globalization. One party calls for relaxed labor standards and increased flexibility e.g. with respect to wages, while the adversaries argue that regulation and harmonization of labor standards are needed in order to cope with the negative effects. Trade unions have to change their strategies if they are to incorporate workers involved in the contracting out of tasks as well as those active in the informal sector. In this they may be helped by the new information technology and the emergence of global work norms. As far as South Africa is concerned Webster calls upon the country to do three things: ensure that the state, and not the market, is at the helm, develop national and regional institutions to make sure that agreements and commitments work properly and, finally, ensure domestic political stability and consensus solutions in politics. This would make a benign hegemonization process possible in southern Africa. Finally, on the market side, to reduce dependence on the outside, more attention must be paid to the role of internal demand.

***

Africa is maintaining its specificity. It could easily become just a global suburb, especially as far as the economy is concerned. But things are not as simple as that. The African nations struggle to find their own ways of participating in global development, making positive use of what the current wave of globalization has to offer and in addition making their own imprint on it. The struggle may be a long and uphill one, but there is no way around it.

2. The African Debacle: The Place of Africa in the Global Economy[1]

Mats Lundahl and Natalie Pienaar

Globalization: New or Old?

Most people, consciously or unconsciously, tend to think of globalization as a recent phenomenon. We are in the middle of a revolution of the technology of information which in the end may prove to have consequences for the world economy that are at least as strong and important as those of the Industrial Revolution of the eighteenth and nineteenth centuries, possibly even stronger and more important. With the advent of such devices as the mobile cellular telephone and the internet the world has shrunk considerably in the mind of the ordinary citizens of most countries of the industrialized west. Capital moves across national boundaries in fractions of a second. Technologies spread across the world. The members of the present young generation travel a great deal more internationally than did their parents. Young university graduates contemplate an international career far more actively than their colleagues just a couple of decades ago. The manufacturing industry tends to be a great deal more footloose than ever before. National economic policies to a much larger extent than hitherto must take into account international factors and the interdependence of economies.

But is this a correct view of globalization? Was the world in some sense 'national', 'regional' or 'local' before? Once the question is posed in this way, the answer, we would argue, is far from self-evident. Of course, it was *more* 'national', 'regional' or 'local', but does that necessarily mean that globalization is a recent phenomenon?

Businessmen, engineers or economists rarely bother with history, but perhaps they should, since it makes far more sense to argue that globalization is a *process* rather than a *state*. Once you view it as a process, the perspective automatically becomes longer.

When did globalization 'begin' then? Some recent works by Kevin O'Rourke and Jeffrey Williamson (1999, 2000, 2002) argue that it is not possible to talk about a genuinely 'global' economy in a way that makes sense until the 'golden age' of international trade and factor movements between 1870 and 1914, since it is not until then that we find anything that resembles commodity and factor price convergence

1. Thanks are due, for constructive comments, to Arne Bigsten, Steven Friedman, Lieb Loots, Nick McNally and Christine Oppong

across a vast geographical region: the Atlantic. This is conspicuously absent during earlier periods of world history.

Other researchers want to go further back. In his three-volume work on the 'modern world-system' Immanuel Wallerstein (1974, 1980, 1989) begins his investigations in sixteenth-century Europe, which remained the 'core' of the system for centuries to come – a core which systematically exploited a periphery consisting of the New World, Asia and Africa. Emphasizing that globalization is a process and taking the age of geographical explorations as a symbolic starting point it is of course as easy to argue Wallerstein's case as that of O'Rourke and Williamson, especially if it is taken into account that one of the principal modes of contact between civilizations and world regions has always been that of aggression, war and conquest. With this view the eventual convergence of prices becomes a subsidiary issue – one belonging to a later period.

One does, however, not have to stop in the age of exploration. Janet Abu-Lughod (1989) accepts Wallerstein's world-system approach but argues that it was preceded by a different type of (world) system: a 'horizontal' one where Europe and Islam were interacting with the Far East from approximately 1250 to about 1350 through 'egalitarian' long-distance trade with positive effects for all parties. The system was destroyed when the 'Pax Mongolica' came to an end with the fall of the Mongol empire in the mid-fourteenth century.

At this point it should be clear that hunting for the 'true' starting point of 'globalization' easily brings us into a search which has a lot in common with Winnie the Pooh's hunt for the heffalump or Pippi Longstocking's hunt for the spunk. What should be considered the appropriate moment simply depends on what you are after. Abu-Lughod's word is of course not the last one in the debate either. Ancient Rome carried on long-distance trade with the peoples around the Indian Ocean and some of these peoples traded further east – all the way to China. Was this in some sense a proto-globalization episode? Was bronze-age Europe part of a world-system (Kristiansen, 1998)? Was there a world system around 3000 BC (Frank, 1993)? The answers partly depend on why the questions are posed and what we expect to get out of asking them.

Be that as it may. We will drop the issue here. What is indisputable is that the present-day world is far more *global* than it has been during any other historical period – as a result of the *globalization processes* of the past.

'Modern' Globalization

Let us concede 'half a point' to O'Rourke and Williamson and accept that 'modern' globalization began during the 1870-1914 period. That period was an era of relatively free trade and factor movements, the advent of the Great Depression reversed this trend. Protectionism carried the day. The passing of the Hawley-Smoot Tariff

Act in the United States in 1930 let loose a wave of retaliatory tariffs elsewhere (Kindleberger, 1986, pp. 123–24). Trade barriers rose and world imports contracted from 2,998 million US gold dollars in January 1929 to 944 million in February 1933 (Kindleberger, 1986, p. 170). However, by 1934 governments began to realize that reciprocal trade liberalization could result in welfare gains. The United States adopted the Reciprocal Trade Agreement Act, and reciprocity and most favored nation status became important elements of the world trade regime (Kindleberger, 1986, pp. 233–35).

World War II led to new disruptions of trade and factor movements but once the war was over, the two principles were turned into the main building blocks of the General Agreement on Tariffs and Trade (GATT), concluded in 1947 among 23 countries (Kenwood and Lougheed, 1999, pp. 241–42) – two of them African (South Africa and Southern Rhodesia) – and of GATT's successor, the World Trade Organization (WTO), formed in 1995, by 127 member countries (Kenwood and Lougheed, 1999, p. 295). As a result of these efforts the distrust and pessimism of the interwar period has today been replaced by a multilateral forum of negotiation.

In addition the world has witnessed an increase in the number of regional trading blocs: for example, the European Union (EU), the North American Free Trade Area (NAFTA), the Association of South East Asian Nations (ASEAN), Mercosur in the southern cone of South America and the Southern African Development Community (SADC). While the debate regarding whether such regional trading blocs are mainly trade creating (substituting cheaper imports for costly domestic production) or trade diverting (substituting more expensive products produced inside the bloc for cheaper products from outside suppliers) there is no doubt that the degree of economic integration within each of these regional blocs is higher than before.

Integration has taken other forms than trade agreements as well. Thus in the 1960s foreign investment regimes were liberalized in many countries, and this was followed by financial liberalization as most of the western industrialized economies began to deregulate their domestic financial sectors. Since the mid-1980s the pace of financial internationalization has been phenomenal. The 1960s also saw the beginning of drastic advances in the internationalization of technology, transport and communication.

All this, together with the multilateral trading system, facilitated the increased flow of commodities, capital and labor across international borders. Furthermore, there is the influence exerted by the 'Bretton Woods' organizations' – the World Bank group and the International Monetary Fund (IMF) – when it comes to imposing homogeneity in economic policy making across the developing world: what is often referred to as the 'Washington Consensus', i.e. the adoption of deregulation and liberal, open economic policies based on the market. Since the collapse of Communism at the beginning of the 1990s very few countries have not moved in the direction of liberalization and deregulation. This includes such politically dictatorial regimes as China and Vietnam – nations that a little more than a decade ago stood out as staunch advocates of regulation and planning.

Is Globalization Good for You?

At this point we must, briefly, raise the question of whether globalization is 'good' or 'bad' for a country. In one sense, the answer depends on your preferences – but not entirely. If we base the judgement on the value premise that globalization is good if it contributes to economic development and bad if it acts as an obstacle to development, we are on somewhat firmer ground. Using a standard definition (Meier, 1995, p. 7), economic development may be defined as sustained growth of real GDP or GNP per capita, provided that the distribution of income does not become more unequal and the number of 'absolute' poor (somehow defined) does not increase. Given this, the question boils down to whether globalization increases growth, reduces income inequalities and reduces poverty, or not.

Globalization, in turn, is concerned with increased flows of commodities, services, factors of production, technologies and information across national boundaries. This is hardly the place to review the debate on how these factors affect the three components in the definition of development. A recent book that deals directly with the issue offers the following 'executive summary' (McCulloch, Winters and Cirera, 2001, p. xxi):

> In general, trade liberalization is an ally in the fight against poverty: it tends to increase average incomes, providing more resources with which to tackle poverty. And while it will generally affect income distribution, it does not appear to do so in a systematically adverse way. Nevertheless, it is important to recognise that most trade reforms will hurt someone, possibly pushing them into, or deeper into, poverty, and that some reforms may increase overall poverty even while they boost incomes in total. Thus, despite the general presumption in favour of trade liberalization, there remain important public policy questions of how to implement it in a way that maximizes its benefits for poverty alleviation and what to do about any poverty that it does create or exacerbate.

Similar capsule statements can be made with respect to movements of factors, technologies and information, but the above will have to do for our present purpose. Critics of free trade and factor movements are usually content just to point out that some of the effects of globalization may not be positive, notably those connected with the cost of transition from a relatively closed to a relatively open economy. This is clearly insufficient. A complete counterfactual must be presented. One cannot simply postulate that no change is better than change – that everything will be fine and dandy in the status quo position.

What happens in the opposite scenario, that of a movement from an open to a closed economy? Would the nations of the third world be better off 'delinking' from the world economy, following the example of North Korea instead of that of South

Korea? We find this extremely hard to believe. Textbooks in international economics are virtually unanimous when it comes to preaching the virtues of free trade and factor movements, and the historical experience backs them on this point. The golden era of free trade and factor movements is the 1870-1914 period, a period when real incomes rose and factor incomes converged in large areas of the globe, as a result of 'globalization' (cf. e.g. O'Rourke and Williamson, 1999).

However, the textbooks never toot the horn of trade and factor movement liberalization without making qualifications. For example, during the period of transition from a closed to an open economy some producers and factors gain while others are hurt, but the way to handle this is not reversing the liberalization process. The remedy has to be sought in domestic policy. The gains that arise from liberalization can be shared if suitable redistribution policies are implemented, and one should not blame liberalization itself if governments fail to step in with the right palliatives.

It is precisely in this light that we have to view globalization. It offers possibilities – but it is up to the different governments to realize them. A golden rule of economic policy states that it is seldom possible to realize more than one goal employing just one means. Each target requires its own instrument. This is in the best case forgotten, in the worst case neglected, by the critics of globalization. It goes without saying that globalization is no panacea. Globalization can contribute to economic development only when supported by adequate domestic policies. It opens the door for development, but governments implementing faulty policies may quickly close that door again.

The present essay is concerned with the extent to which economic globalization has been felt in Africa. Currently it is clear that Africa is marginalized in the world economy. It is a global spectator rather than an active global player. What are the main reasons for this? Have any attempts been made to come to grips with them? Is there any evidence that this trend may be reversed? In order to gain some insights into these issues we will begin by an overview of some important globalization trends. Thereafter we will present Africa's marginal role in the world economy. This is followed by a discussion of the factors that have contributed to the marginalization and of the attempts that have been made to reform the structures responsible. Finally we will look at some measures that are necessary if Africa is to be ensured a role as a more important active global player in the future.

Some Facts

From 1980 to 2000 the volume of world merchandise exports increased by 188%, and manufacturing exports (the fastest-growing sector) by no less than 262%. Agricultural exports increased by 79%, and mining exports by 64%. Altogether world exports grew faster than world output: 3 times as fast in the case of total exports, 3.6 times for manufactures, 1.4 times for agriculture, and 3.8 times for mining products

(WTO, 2001, Table II.1). Between the early 1970s and the late 1990s the ratio of world exports to world output increased from one to eight to almost one to five (Nayyar, 2000, p. 5).

A similar increase took place in the world flow of foreign direct investment – a fourfold increase between 1990 and 1999, and between 1980 and 1996 the stock of foreign direct investment in relation to world output increased from less than 5% to more than 10% (Nayyar, 2000, p. 5). Foreign direct investment – both outflows and inflows – concentrates heavily on the developed economies, although this dominance has decreased over time. Thus, between 1975 and 1977 developed countries accounted for 98% of the outflows and 69% of the inflows (Rasiah, 2000, p. 944). Twenty-three years later (1998-2000) the former share had fallen to 93% while the latter had risen to 76% (UNCTAD, 2001a, p. 3). During the same period, the inflow share of developing countries decreased from 31% to 21%, while on the outflow side there was an increase from 1.4% 1975–77 to 7% 1998–2000. The rise of outflows was a consequence of the rapid development of such countries as South Korea, Taiwan and Singapore in Southeast Asia (Rasiah, 2001, pp. 944–45). The inflows, in turn, have been concentrated to 'resource-rich economies that are fairly politically stable, endowed with good infrastructure and demonstrate governance structures that are relatively capital-friendly. Low-wage unskilled labour is important, but is available as a ubiquitous resource in a number of developing economies' (Rasiah, 2001, p. 945).

The most staggering development has taken place in the field of international finance where global foreign exchange transactions increased from US$ 60 billion per day in 1983 to 1,500 billion in 1997. By comparison, the latter year world GDP per day was 82 billion per day, world exports 16 billion per day and the foreign exchange reserves of all central banks 1,550 billion (Nayyar, 2000, p. 5).

The African Debacle

Where is Africa in all this? Unfortunately, the answer is: 'lagging behind'. Excluding South Africa, the total income of Sub-Saharan Africa amounts to a little more than that of Denmark – to be split among 48 nations (World Bank, 2001, pp. 274–75). The performance of most African economies during the last few decades leaves a lot to be desired. In 1950 GNP per capita for Africa south of the Sahara amounted to 11% of that of the OECD countries. In 1989 the figure had fallen to 5% (World Bank, 1991, p. 14). In terms of growth Africa has performed a great deal worse than Latin America or Asia. During the 1980s GDP per capita in the African countries declined by on average 1.3% per annum (Collier and Gunning, 1999a. p. 64). Today average GDP per capita in Africa is lower than in 1970 (World Bank, 2000, p. 8).

At the end of the 1980s the African economies were in crisis – a crisis that would continue in the 1990s. Exports had failed to expand rapidly enough to allow the debt that had accumulated to be paid off. The African share of world (or for that matter third world) exports fell from the 1950s to the beginning of the 1990s, and few Sub-Saharan countries could boast a sustained growth of export revenue in the 1980s. The debt burden grew to the point where at the end of the decade it equaled the GNP of the region – a record not matched by any other region in the world, and at the beginning of the 1990s half the Sub-Saharan export revenues were mortgaged to service the foreign debt (Stymne, 1993), and at the end of 1997 the foreign debt on average amounted to more than 80% of GDP. Africa was the only major economic region in the world where investment and savings per capita declined after 1970. The average savings rate – 13% of GDP – was the lowest in the world in the 1990s (World Bank, 2000, p. 9).

The exceptions to the bad record were few. In 1995 only 6% of the population of Sub-Saharan Africa was found in countries whose per capita income was higher than ever before (Freeman and Lindauer, 1999, pp. 2, 27). The optimism that characterized the new African nations at the time of their independence in the 1960s was by and large gone, as it was realized that the continent was undergoing a process of economic decline.

Between 1990 and 1994 the rate of decline had accelerated to 1.8% on a yearly basis (Collier and Gunning, 1999a, p. 64). The latter half of the 1990s saw a recovery, with an average growth rate of GDP of 4.3% 1994-98 (World Bank, 2000, p. 33), but the African performance still remained weak in a comparative perspective. Taking the decade as a whole, the fastest growing region in the world between 1990 and 1999 was East Asia and the Pacific, with an average GDP growth rate of 7.4%, followed by South Asia with 5.7%, while the figure for Sub-Saharan Africa was 2.4%, less than Latin America and the Caribbean and the Middle East and North Africa (World Bank, 2001, p. 295).

Of course, the experiences differed. Botswana and Mauritius had a rapid and steady growth rate, and countries like Cameroon, Gabon, Côte d'Ivoire, Nigeria and Togo also had periods of high growth, while the figures for Benin, Chad and Madagascar were steadily negative. However, the typical pattern was one of an initial economic expansion, followed by stagnation or decline. The African economies failed to get on to *sustained* growth paths. Most countries reached the point of stagnation or decline between 1972 and 1982, and after 1973 physical capital accumulation almost collapsed. It was close to zero from this date up to 1994, negative 1984-94 (Ndulu and O'Connell, 1999, pp. 42, 45). Thereafter a recovery set in. The growth rate of gross domestic investment in sub-Saharan Africa between 1990 and 1999 was 3.6% per annum on average (World Bank 2001, p. 295).

Africa is marginalized in terms of exports and imports as well. At present a dozen developing countries account for about 70% of the exports from the third world (Nayyar, 2000, p. 10). Sub-Saharan Africa's share of world exports in 1990 was a mere 1.9%. Ten years later the figure had fallen to 1.3%. Similarly its share of world imports had shrunk from 1.7% to 1.6% (World Bank, 2001, p. 303). The loss of world trade shares is, however, not a phenomenon only of the 1990s. Extending the picture backwards leads to an amazing conclusion. The decline of Africa's share of world exports from 1970 to 1993 represents a loss of no less than US$ 68 billion every year, or the equivalent of 21% of the regional GDP (World Bank, 2000, p. 20).

Capital flows present a similar picture. The same dozen nations that dominate third world exports also absorb about 80% of the investment flows to the developing world (Nayyar, 2000, p. 10). Africa has failed to share in the recovery of private capital flows to emerging markets in the 1990s and the flows that do go into Africa are more volatile and short-term than flows going elsewhere (UNCTAD, 2000, p. 11). According to UNCTAD (2001a, p. 3) figures, all of Africa accounted for less than 1% of the total foreign direct investment inflow 1998–2000. This represents a decline compared to the figure for 1989–94: 2%.

This reduction has largely been due to a dramatic decrease of private flows and bank lending to the region after the financial crisis in the 1980s. Foreign direct investment is furthermore very unevenly distributed across Africa. About 65 per cent of the total inflow 1997–98 centred on South Africa, Nigeria and Côte d'Ivoire (Morisset, 2000, p. 4). Africa in general has not shared in the increase of the activities of multinational corporations and the spread of production across borders. The continent mainly attracts companies like Shell in Nigeria, i.e. activities that are driven by the availability of natural resources. The general level of productivity is too low and the manufacturing sectors are too small and underdeveloped to allow Africa to receive any significant inflows of foreign direct investment.

To sum up, it is clear that Africa is a marginal region in the world economy. World output, trade and foreign direct investment have all increased during the past decades, but Africa is lagging behind.

Why Is Africa Marginalized?

While the bad performance is beyond dispute (cf., however, Sender, 1999, for a dissenting opinion), when it comes to the causes, views differ considerably. Many governments have had a tendency to emphasize external factors: the oil price rise induced by OPEC in 1973, the macroeconomic stabilization problems that would follow, the recession in the international economy 1974–75 and another oil price shock beginning in 1978 that resulted in a new recession in 1981–82 all undoubtedly contributed to the debt crisis that began to make itself felt in 1982–83 and culminated in the mid–1980s. By then it had wreaked havoc among oil exporting and oil importing countries alike (Cooper, 1992, Ch. 1, 4). According to UNCTAD (2001b, pp. 35–36), the continued deterioration of Africa's terms of trade during the 1980s and 1990s served to cut the continent's share of world exports in half and reduce the GDP per capita level in 1997 by no less than one-third.

The fact that virtually all the African countries 'export primary commodities, and most export little else' (Deaton, 1999, p. 23) has thus been the subject of much concern. It has been argued that these products are unsuitable for serving as the foundation for growth and development strategies. Economies lacking natural resources have a tendency to grow faster, not slower, than economies that are resource abundant (Auty, 1993, 2001). There is always the risk of Dutch Disease: that the inflow of foreign exchange from primary exports serves to appreciate the domestic currency to the point where the manufacturing sector gets into trouble, and primary exports, notably of minerals, may have only weak forward and backward linkage effects. Mineral rents are also easy to tax, and unless the revenue is spent wisely – not squandered by the ruling groups – the impact on growth and development may be small. Finally, commodity booms tend to lead to increased government spending which in turn causes trouble when the downswing comes. Basing a 'grand development strategy' on primary products does not seem recommendable. It is difficult to find genuine staple products (Findlay and Lundahl, 1994, 2001) with strong linkage effects, but in the African case it is hardly possible to escape from the fact that primary production is likely to be very important also in the foreseeable future (Deaton, 1999, pp. 38–39):

> Natural resources are as abundant in Africa as human capital is scarce, and Africa is likely to have a comparative advantage in exports of primary products for many years to come ... The volatility of export incomes makes life difficult for policymakers, but not by enough so that they should consider abandoning the enterprise. African economies would be better off if commodity prices were higher, but there is surely little prospect that future cartels will be any more successful than those that have tried and failed in the past. The roots of Africa's slow development almost certainly lie elsewhere ...

The bad performance of the African economies has not only, and not even primarily, been a result of external circumstances – circumstances beyond the control of African policy makers. Far from that. It has been directly related to faulty policy. A systematic recent survey of the African economies, by Collier and Gunning, concludes (Collier and Gunning, 1999a, p. 100):

> Africa stagnated because its governments were captured by a narrow elite that undermined markets and used public services to deliver employment patronage. These policies reduced the returns on assets and increased the already high risks private agents faced. To cope, private agents moved both financial and human capital abroad and diverted their social capital into risk-reduction and risk-bearing mechanisms.

The degree of ethno-linguistic fractionalization is a great deal higher in Africa than in other parts of the world, and in countries where democratic political rights have been lacking, this has had a negative impact on growth, directly and through the impact of faulty policies designed to further the interests of particular groups rather than the national interest (Easterly and Levine, 1997). The 'commanding heights' were effectively isolated from the populations at large and when they formulated their policies they responded only to the signals sent out by whatever factions they represented.

Some of these policies were directly connected with globalization. Export agriculture became a source of funds for industrial expansion, via extensive taxation, except in the cases where the rulers and the political elite themselves had a direct interest in favouring export agriculture. The direct squeeze of export agriculture was supported by the creation of an indirect anti-export bias: the channelling of credits via the banking system to the manufacturing sector. The measures did not fail to have an impact (Collier and Gunning, 1999a, p. 68): 'These anti-export policies were widely adopted between the mid-1960s and the mid-1970s. In some countries their effects were temporarily disguised by the commodity booms of 1975–79, but by the early 1980s most African economies were declining.'

There was, however, more that the state could do to damage exports. Many African economies turned inwards by resorting to import substitution in manufacturing, either by erecting high tariff walls, or by employing quantitative import restrictions. These measures, which served to reallocate resources away from production for export, were complemented with foreign exchange controls that punished exporters and made it difficult – often impossible – for them to keep the foreign exchange they had earned. Another generalized pattern was the creation of parastatal agricultural marketing boards which in combination with the imposition of price controls served to drive a wedge between world market prices and the prices received by African producers (World Bank, 1982, Part II, Krueger, Schiff and Valdés, 1991). Production for exports was taxed, and the kind of incentive goods that would have made it worthwhile for farmers to produce for export was often not available (Bevan, Collier and Gunning, 1989).

If all the policy measures damaging trade are taken into consideration the African economies stood out as much more closed than those of other regions of the world. Africa had by far the highest trade restrictions and the relatively small size of the African economies made the restrictions more damaging than elsewhere.

Exchange rates were frequently out of line with reality. Currencies were overvalued, with the result that tariffs and quantitative import restrictions had to be imposed in order to prevent acute balance of payments problems. In the end devaluation had to be resorted to but often failed to be effective since as long as domestic price controls continued the governments failed to get prices right. Supplementary inputs like credits were not made available and when macroeconomic stabilization was not undertaken exports did not receive any stimulus.

A factor that affected not just exports, but economic life in general, was the lack of public service. African economies generally display a higher ratio of public expenditure to GDP than economies elsewhere in the world. However, most of the expenditure consists of wages and salaries, and as a result of this the public infra-structure, e.g. telecommunications and transportation, suffers. The return to public investment falls and it becomes difficult for the private sector to carry out its work efficiently, i.e. the lack of public service acts as a deterrent to private investment (Collier and Gunning, 1999a, pp. 70–75).

So does presumably deficient financial intermediation. African economies fre-quently give the impression of pursuing 'shallow' strategies. Banks were often social-ized and were used to channel funds into an ailing parastatal sector instead of to ensure that savings found their way into the most high-yielding private sector projects. This also served to stimulate corrupt lending. Both practices contributed to a high incidence of defaults. When private banks were allowed they were often heavily taxed – even more so than exports – by harsh reserve requirements. Limiting the number of banks created oligopolies and high lending costs (Collier and Gun-ning, 1999a, pp. 90–92). Against this background it hardly comes as a surprise to learn that the capital flight from Africa has been rampant. In 1990 no less than 39 per cent of the portfolios of African wealth owners were held outside the continent – a figure as high as the one for the notorious Middle East and far higher than those for Latin America or Asia (Collier and Gunning, 1999a, pp. 92–93).

Policies that destroyed markets were not limited to exports and banking, but per-meated product markets as well. Well-meaning or ideological governments decided that it was best to abolish private middlemen in the marketing of agricultural pro-duce, since the middlemen exploited the consumers. Inefficient parastatals were substituted for them, prices and quantities were regulated and trade between differ-ent geographical territories was prohibited (World Bank, 2000, 25). All this consti-tuted a certain recipe for disaster. Agricultural producers received a fraction of what they would have got in a competitive market, payment was frequently delayed and the inputs that were to be supplied via the crop parastatals reached the farmers late, if at all. The situation began to resemble that prevailing in the Communist countries of Eastern Europe, with high trading costs, shortages, black markets, inefficient allocation of resources and high risks. Where pan-territorial pricing (the same price everywhere, without any regard for transport costs) was resorted to huge surpluses piled up in distant, inaccessible regions.

The extreme degree of 'dirigisme' that characterized the African economies for two or three decades served as a very efficient obstacle to integration in the world economy. Between 1990 and 1994 the return on foreign direct investment in Africa was about 60 per cent higher than in other areas of the third world. Yet less than 2 per cent of the investment flows to developing countries went to Africa. The conti-nent was clearly perceived as a high-risk area by foreign investors (Collier and Gun-ning, 1999a, pp. 103–04). It stood out as utterly peripheral in the global economy.

Reform Attempts

There remain few doubts as to why Africa was a marginal player in the globalization game in the mid-1990s. The policies carried out during most of the post-independence period did not qualify her for any other role. Through a number of measures governments across the continent had more or less destroyed the growth-creating mechanisms of their economies, substituted awkward administrative decision procedures for markets and encouraged the furthering of the welfare of the few at the expense of the many.

During this process, however, events signalling that everything was not well had not failed to present themselves. Macroeconomic imbalances, huge foreign debts and low productivity in general indicated that the African economies were ripe for reform. The reform experience, however, has been very mixed, to say the least. This point may be illustrated with some examples from African countries receiving Swedish assistance (Lundahl, 2001).

Of the twelve most important recipients four belong to the category of recently war-stricken countries: Angola, Guinea-Bissau, Ethiopia and Eritrea. These countries have opted for guns instead of butter and all of them had at some point chosen a marxist-leninist development strategy. (The case of Mozambique is similar, although the war there ended in 1992.) The economic history of Angola during the 1990s can be summarized by just four words: civil war and mismanagement. No serious reform attempts have been made. Political unrest has blocked them. Guinea-Bissau, Ethiopia and Eritrea all began reform programs but once the wars were on they were interrupted. The road chosen did not lead ahead but back. It is estimated that one of every five Africans lives in countries either formally at war or otherwise disrupted by conflict that, on average, lowers growth by 2 percentage points per annum (World Bank, 2000, p. 40).

A second group of countries may be labelled reform strugglers: Kenya, Cape Verde, Zambia, Tanzania, Mozambique and Zimbabwe. These countries have to varying degrees implemented structural adjustment and stabilization programs. Their experience varies as well, but they have one important feature in common. All of them have shown a lack of political willingness to implement changes and once the hour of reform arrived the conversion took place under the gallows. The measures carried out were half-hearted and it was with great reluctance that the decision to launch them was taken. Frequently the desire was to continue the *ancien régime*, and as a result a stop-go cycle of economic policy was initiated (cf. Krueger, 1995, p. 89).

This was understandable since setting up a system that builds on centralization of command, administrative decisions, rent creation and rent seeking provides hosts of opportunities for those in power to enrich themselves. The very institutions that are needed in order to put an end to inefficiency and corruption are never created.

Four of the six reform struggler countries are included in the latest issue of the Transparency International Corruption Perception Index (Transparency International, 2001) – all of them at the bottom of the ladder of 91 countries, with Kenya ranking number 84, Tanzania 82, Zambia 75 and Zimbabwe 65, with scores ranging from 2.0 in the case of Kenya to 2.6 for Zimbabwe. (A score of 10 indicates a highly 'clean' country and one of 0 a highly corrupt. The index for the least corrupt country, Finland, was 9.9 and the most corrupt of the Nordic countries, Norway, had a score of 8.6. A level below 5 is considered an indication of high levels of corruption.)

The final three countries on the list – Uganda, South Africa and Lesotho – may be viewed as growth seekers, i.e. as countries that have undertaken policy and institutional reform and which should now be growing steadily if the reforms have been successful. On average, however, the results are below expectations, for largely different reasons. Uganda has not reached the point where growth is sustained. The investment rate is too low, the country is still dependent on aid and the growth of manufacturing remains sluggish. South Africa has failed to reach a growth rate which steadily outstrips that of the population. The 'engine of growth' is difficult to find, and none of the strategies proposed stands out as panacea in this respect. Prospective investors lack a confidence in the future that is strong enough to make them act. Lesotho, finally, has experienced high growth over a few years, for reasons that, however, will cease to be present in the future, notably the huge Lesotho Highlands Water Project, the completion of which will make continued growth a great deal more difficult to achieve.

Our examples illustrate the general point that in spite of the reforms of the 1990s Africa has not yet reached the point where it is possible to talk about sustained growth. On the contrary, it may be argued that the continent is still in precarious economic shape, with elements of crisis still present in many countries. By the very same token Africa remains on the periphery of the world economy. The intensified globalization of the 1990s has by and large passed the continent by.

This does not amount to saying that reforms have had no impact (World Bank, 2000, pp. 28–37). Fiscal deficits have been reduced, inflation has come down and tax bases have been broadened in many countries. Most prices have been decontrolled, black market premiums on foreign currency have been reduced substantially, taxes on foreign trade have been brought down and tariff levels have been unified. Private economic initiative has been given a more prominent role and privatization of government enterprises has accelerated in many countries. However, as our examples illustrate, many countries have moved in and out of commitment to reform – giving the latter too little time to work. On the other hand, sustained reform in combination with external financial assistance has produced fairly satisfactory results.

Can Africa Enter the Globalization Game as an Active Player?

Will it be possible for Africa to enter the globalization process in a more active way than hitherto? All observers do not agree with the statement that African economic performance has been bad in the past. Thus, John Sender (1999) argues that indicators related to basic needs show that Africa is much better off today than fifty years ago and directly contradict figures about falling crop production that are reported from time to time. Compound figures for 1965–1996 instead indicate steady agricultural growth.

This clearly points towards a role for Africa in the world economy, but Sender is sceptical, to say the least, to the orthodox view that builds on the IMF variety of stabilization policy and liberation of the market forces. Following the standard recipe has not resulted in higher growth and a larger inflow of foreign capital. On the contrary, investment rates have tended to decline instead. Sender is sceptical also towards the 'post-Washington consensus' suggested by Joseph Stiglitz (1998) which holds that governments have an important role to play in the correction of market failures, but that states should not overstretch beyond their capabilities. He points toward the possibility of 'institutional learning', argues that industrialization is decisive for economic development and suggests that selective government intervention in key import substitution and export-oriented industries is warranted: protection and subsidization.

It is, however, doubtful whether the strategy suggested by Sender would enable Africa to play a more active role in the international economy. It is difficult to escape from the impression that it amounts to turning inwards again, under a government umbrella: precisely the same recipe that produced disaster from the 1960s. But what exactly is the role that trade may play? Africa is marginalized in the international economy because the economies of the continent fail to grow, but is openness itself a prerequisite for growth? It hardly seems that the African economies have abnormally low ratios of trade to GDP for their income level, size and geographical location. Also, it cannot be denied that the majority of the African states south of the Sahara have during recent years moved in the direction of more, not less, trade, without visible results (Freeman and Lindauer, 1999).

But if neither openness (in stark contrast to theory) nor its opposite promotes growth, then clearly other considerations must be more important (Collier and Gunning, 1999b, pp. 18–19). Are there any circumstances which serve to constrain the African economies in such a way as to preclude whatever beneficial effects international trade may have from coming into play? Or, to put it slightly differently, are there any measures that must be implemented before the African economies can get into a virtuous spiral of increased openness and higher growth?

An obvious candidate is democratization. Much depends on the quality of government. African political regimes typically developed in three phases after independence: consolidation of authoritarian rule during the 1970s, crisis management by these regimes in the following decade and a shift towards democracy from around 1990 (Ndulu and O'Connell, 1999, p. 45). In 1988 only Botswana, The Gambia, Mauritius, Senegal and Zimbabwe had multi-party systems. The remaining 42 nations of sub-Saharan Africa could be divided into 11 military oligarchies, 16 plebiscitary one-party systems, 13 competitive one-party systems and two settler oligarchies (Namibia and South Africa). Even without entering into any details of definitions, it is easily seen that democracy was not the rule. As, however, domestic protests began to mount, 33 of the 42 countries increased the extent of civil liberties between 1988 and 1992, and two years later 16 countries had held democratic elections (Bratton and van de Walle, 1997). The extent of political participation has increased sharply during the past ten years, which in turn may pave the way for more accountable and responsible governments in Africa. Since the early 1990s the vast majority of the countries south of the Sahara have held multi-party presidential or parliamentary elections (Mbendi, 2001) The road towards democracy has been trodden.

Far less encouraging is that a number of countries, like Angola, the Democratic Republic of Congo, Rwanda and the Sudan, are still involved in wars or internal conflicts, involving a number of neighbouring states as well. Governance is bad in all these instances and the war-stricken countries have massive macroeconomic problems, problems that will have to be addressed together with the issue of structural adjustment, once the bellicose activities have come to an end.

To what extent democratization will serve to boost growth remains to be seen. In a recent paper, Benno Ndulu and Stephen O'Connell (1999, p. 41) draw the following conclusion:

> It would be premature to conclude that Africa's political reforms of the 1990s have helped to generate economic progress. However, we believe that the increase in political pluralism, in combination with greater unity among African aid donors, bodes well for a continuation of Africa's growth recovery.

Hopefully, they are right, but political democracy alone is not likely to do the growth trick.

Another way forward that has frequently been suggested goes via education (World Bank, 2000, Ch. 4). However, as it seems, the crucial role of education for economic growth that is postulated in many of the so-called endogenous growth models (cf. e.g. Aghion and Howitt, 1998, Ch. 10) is not at all borne out by empirical studies of Africa (Freeman and Lindauer, 1999). In particular, primary education, which has indeed expanded in Africa, does not seem to have any impact on growth. Secondary and tertiary education score better, possibly because its quality is better than that of primary education, comparatively speaking. Physical capital performs better than human capital in macroeconomic regression studies, and on the human capital side health factors may have been more limiting for growth than education (Schultz, 1999). Exactly as in the case of openness it may be other constraints than schooling that are binding (Freeman and Lindauer, 1999, p. 6):

> ... the return to schooling requires stable property relations and a safe economic environment, which have been lacking in most African states. Wars, corruption, revolutions, and other instabilities that disturb or distort the normal functioning of markets make the value of schooling less than it would be in a more stable world.

Of course, schooling may have a number of indirect effects that are beneficial for growth. If directed towards women it serves to reduce the mortality of both the women themselves and their children. Education may be instrumental in fostering democracy as well. Also, education may be necessary as physical capital of newer vintages accumulates. Thus, investment in education should not be discarded.

On the human side we cannot forget about HIV and AIDS either. Many African countries are in the situation where life expectancy may be reduced by as much as twenty years while at the same time the work force will be decimated. This will have an impact both on output and on social costs in ways that we still know very little about. Neglecting the AIDS problem or tackling it too late may amount to paying a terribly high price (cf. the articles in the *Journal of International Development*, 2001). Unfortunately, political commitment is lacking in far too many African countries.

Economic policies also matter. Stabilization and structural adjustment are necessary components if Africa is to experience a renaissance and play a more active role in the international economy than hitherto. Risk capital will not find its way to economies that are out of joint. The African governments must offer a stable policy environment built on market principles if their economies are to move on to sustained growth paths with increases in real GDP or GNP per capita steadily outstripping the growth of the population. Industry and trade policies that build on comparative advantage must be put in place. The industrial push initiated in the 1960s failed precisely because it ignored these principles.

Stabilization and structural adjustment are not enough, however. Reginald Herbold Green (1998) has stressed that a number of African economies, like Ghana, Tanzania, Uganda, Namibia, South Africa and Ethiopia, have successfully implemented structural adjustment programs and innovative domestic policies. This has led to fiscal, monetary and external stabilization and to the restoration of modest economic growth. They, however, still have to combat such evils as corruption and inefficiency in government. The African economies also need diversification. Africa is urbanizing very rapidly, but its economies essentially remain agricultural, with the result that employment and incomes suffer. Altogether, the list of what has to be done is long. Unfortunately there is no 'shortcut to progress'. Only when all the issues dealt with in the present essay are addressed are we likely to see what Arne

Bigsten (1999) has termed African tigers (we prefer lions), with sustained growth rates of 6–10 per cent per annum, emerge.

Conclusions

There is nothing new under the sun – not even globalization. This is a process that has been unfolding for a long period of time. Recently, however, the process has been intensified. The world has shrunk, as it were, as a result of increased international trade and factor movements, as well as the increased ease of spread of technology and information.

The globalization process has affected the third world as much as the first or second, and there is a strong case for arguing that those third world countries that have participated actively in the globalization process and at the same time have actively used domestic policies to complement and facilitate it and, where necessary, forestall or mitigate its negative effects, have fared well, whereas the countries that have resisted globalization and used domestic policies to regulate and petrify the economy have fared badly.

Unfortunately, the African countries, with few exceptions, belong to the latter category. To say that globalization has passed Africa by or that Africa is a marginalized continent in the world economy is to reverse cause and effect. Africa is a passive spectator in the international economic arena among other things because its leaders chose to be passive. They turned Africa inwards, away from the international current of possibilities that gradually unfolded as globalization proceeded. This is one of the main reasons why we have an Asian miracle but an African debacle.

References

Abu-Lughod, Janet L. (1989), *Before European Hegemony*. Oxford: Oxford University Press.

Aghion, Philippe and Peter Howitt (1998), *Endogenous Growth Theory*. Cambridge, MA and London: MIT Press.

Auty, Richard M. (1993), *Sustaining Development in Mineral Economies: The Resource Curse Thesis*. London and New York: Routledge.

Auty, Richard M. (ed.) (2001), *Resource Abundance and Economic Development*. Oxford: Oxford University Press.

Bevan, David, Paul Collier and Jan W. Gunning, with Arne Bigsten and Paul Horsnell (1989), *Peasants and Governments: An Economic Analysis*. Oxford: Clarendon Press.

Bigsten, Arne (1999), "Looking for African Tigers", in Steve Kayizzi-Mugerwa (ed.), *The African Economy: Policy, Institutions and the Future*. London and New York: Routledge.

Bratton, Michael and Nicolas van de Walle (1997), *Democratic Experiments in Africa*. Cambridge: Cambridge University Press.

Collier, Paul and Jan W. Gunning (1999a), "Explaining African Economic Performance", *Journal of Economic Literature*, Vol. 37.

Collier, Paul and Jan W. Gunning (1999b), "Why Has Africa Grown Slowly", *Journal of Economic Perspectives,* Vol. 13.

Cooper, Richard N. (1992), *Economic Stabilization and Debt in Developing Countries.* Cambridge, MA and London: MIT Press.

Deaton, Angus (1999), "Commodity Prices and Growth in Africa", *Journal of Economic Perspectives,* Vol. 13.

Easterly, William and Ross Levine (1997), "Africa's Growth Tragedy: Policies and Ethnic Divisions", *Quarterly Journal of Economics,* Vol. 112.

Findlay, Ronald and Mats Lundahl (1994), "Natural Resources, Vent-for-Surplus, and the Staples Theory", in Gerald M. Meier (ed.), *From Classical Economics to Development Economics.* New York: St. Martin's Press.

Findlay, Ronald and Mats Lundahl (2001), "Natural Resources and Economic Development: The 1870–1914 Experience", in Richard M. Auty (ed.), *Resource Abundance and Economic Development.* Oxford: Oxford University Press.

Frank, Andre Gunder (1993), "Bronze Age World System Cycles", *Current Anthropology,* Vol. 34.

Freeman, Richard B. and David L. Lindauer (1999), "Why Not Africa?", *Working Paper 6942.* Cambridge, MA: National Bureau of Economic Research.

Green, Reginald Herbold (1998), "A Cloth Untrue: The Evolution of Structural Adjustment in Sub-Saharan Africa", *Journal of International Affairs,* Vol. 52.

Journal of International Development (2001), Special Issue: "Aids and Development in Africa". Editors: Simon Dixon, Scott McDonald and Jennifer Roberts. Vol. 13, No. 4, May.

Kenwood, A.G. and A.L. Lougheed (1999), *The Growth of the International Economy 1820–2000. An Introductory Text.* Fourth edition. London and New York: Routledge.

Kindleberger, Charles P. (1986), *The World in Depression, 1929–1939.* Revised and Enlarged Edition. Berkeley, CA: University of California Press.

Kristiansen, Kristian (1998), *Europe before History.* Cambridge: Cambridge University Press.

Krueger, Anne O. (1995), *Political Economy of Policy Reform in Developing Countries.* Cambridge, MA: MIT Press.

Krueger, Anne O., Maurice Schiff and Alberto Valdés (eds) (1991), *The Political Economy of Agricultural Pricing Policy, Vol. 3: Africa and the Mediterranean.* Baltimore and London: Johns Hopkins University Press.

Lundahl, Mats (ed.) (2001), *From Crisis to Growth in Africa?* London and New York: Routledge.

Mbendi Information for Africa (2001), http://www.mbendi.co.za/indy/trad/p0005.htm, 2 July.

McCulloch, Neil, L. Alan Winters and Xavier Cirera (2001), *Trade Liberalization and Poverty: A Handbook.* London: Centre for Economic Policy Research.

Meier, Gerald M. (ed.) (1995), *Leading Issues in Economic Development.* Sixth edition. Oxford: Oxford University Press.

Morisset, Jacques (2000), *Foreign Direct Investment in Africa: Policies Also Matter.* Working Paper No. 2481, Washington DC: World Bank.

Nayyar, Deepak (2000), "Globalization and Development Strategies". Paper prepared for UNCTAD X High-Level Round Table on Trade and Development, Directions for the Twenty-First Century, Bangkok, 12 February.

Ndulu, Benno J. and Stephen A. O'Connell (1999), 'Governance and Growth in Sub-Saharan Africa', *Journal of Economic Perspectives,* Vol. 13.

O'Rourke, Kevin H. and Jeffrey G. Williamson (1999), *Globalization and History. The Evolution of a Nineteenth-Century Atlantic Economy.* Cambridge, MA: MIT Press.

O'Rourke, Kevin H. and Jeffrey G. Williamson (2000), "When Did Globalization Begin?". Mimeo, Cambridge, MA: Department of Economics, Harvard University.

O'Rourke, Kevin H. and Jeffrey G. Williamson (2002), "The Heckscher-Ohlin Model between 1400 and 2000: When It Explained Factor Price Convergence, When It Did Not, and Why", in Ronald Findlay, Lars Jonung and Mats Lundahl (eds.), *Bertil Ohlin: A Centennial Celebration (1899–1999).* Cambridge, MA and London: MIT Press.

Rasiah, Rajah (2000), "Globalization and Private Capital Movements", *Third World Quarterly,* Vol. 21.

Schultz, T. Paul (1999), "Health and Schooling Investments in Africa", *Journal of Economic Perspectives,* Vol. 13.

Sender, John (1999), "Africa's Economic Performance: Limitations of the Current Consensus", *Journal of Economic Perspectives,* Vol. 13.

Stiglitz, Joseph E. (1998), *More Instruments and Broader Goals: Moving toward the Post-Washington Consensus.* Helsinki: UNU World Institute for Development Economics Research (WIDER).

Stymne, Joakim (1993), "Reducing the Debt Burden of Sub-Saharan Africa", in Magnus Blomström and Mats Lundahl (eds.), *Economic Crisis in Africa. Perspectives on Policy Responses.* London and New York: Routledge.

Transparency International (2001), Press Release: "New Index Highlights Worldwide Corruption Crisis", http://www.transparency.org/documents/cpi/2001/cpi2001.html, 27 June.

UNCTAD (United Nations Conference on Trade and Development) (2000), *Capital Flows and Growth in Africa.* New York and Geneva: United Nations.

UNCTAD (2001a), *World Investment Report 2001. Promoting Linkages. Overview.* Internet edition. New York and Geneva: United Nations.

UNCTAD (2001b), *Economic Development in Africa: Performance, Prospects and Policy Issues.* New York and Geneva: United Nations.

Wallerstein, Immanuel (1974), *The Modern World-System I: Capitalist Agriculture and the Origins of the European World-Economy in the Sixteenth Century.* New York: Academic Press.

Wallerstein, Immanuel (1980), *The Modern World-System II: Mercantilism and the Consolidation of the European World-Economy, 1600–1750.* New York: Academic Press.

Wallerstein, Immanuel (1989), *The Modern World-System III: The Second Era of Great Expansion of the Capitalist World-Economy, 1730–1840s.* San Diego, CA: Academic Press.

World Bank (1982), *World Development Report 1982.* New York: Oxford University Press.

World Bank (1991), *World Development Report 1991.* New York: Oxford University Press.

World Bank (2000), *Can Africa Claim the 21st Century?* Washington, DC: World Bank.

World Bank (2001), *World Development Report 2000/2001.* Oxford: Oxford University Press.

WTO (World Trade Organization) (2001), "World Merchandise Exports, Production and Gross Domestic Product, 1950–00", http:www.wto.org/english/res_e/statis_e/its2001_e/section2/ii01.xls.

3. Globalization and Structural Adjustment in Africa

Arne Bigsten and Dick Durevall

Introduction

Globalization has several meanings in the public debate, but the economists' usage tends to refer to the integration of economies with regard to markets for goods, factors of production and technology. By this definition we can identify two recent eras of globalization, namely the one of the late 19th century up to World War I, and the recent epoch covering the last few decades. As far as the most recent era is concerned it is clear that the speed of economic integration has increased. Subramanian and Tamirisa (2001) show that the elasticity of trade flows with respect to distance fell by 30 per cent between 1980 and 1997. Goods flow more easily across the globe than they used to do. This is due to a combination of technological progress, which has lowered transport costs, and improvements in trade related service sectors and trade liberalization measures. It is also notable that the common language dummy in their regressions on trade flows went from significantly positive to insignificant, which may suggest that inter-country contacts are less hindered by language barriers than they used to be.[1]

During this process of international economic integration most parts of the third world have seen considerable economic improvements, while Africa stands out as having been left behind.[2] Global inequality as measured by the Gini coefficient in purchasing power terms has decreased since 1968, but the bottom ten per cent of the distribution has seen its share of the global GDP decline (Melchior, Telle and Wiig, 2000). This category largely comprises Africa. So why has Africa not done better during the recent era of globalization?

Globalization in Sub-Saharan Africa is closely linked to the structural adjustment programmes. Hence, in this chapter we focus on the structural adjustment and interactions between politics and institutional characteristics. In particular, we argue that one important explanation for the dismal performance of many African countries, in spite of the measures taken towards market liberalization, is a lack of willingness or ability on the part of the politicians to respect the restrictions imposed by the liberalised markets. Before structural adjustment, the scope for domestic policy makers was much wider since controls made prices, and hence production and con-

---

1. The dummy for a common border, however, has actually become more significant.
2. In Bigsten (2002), it was argued that African countries during the last twenty years had liberalised their inward-oriented trade regimes, but that the African economies had been marginalized from the international economy in several ways.

sumption, react slowly to changes in policy. However, after liberalization many prices react quickly to policies. Good policymaking is thus more important in a liberalised environment than in one with many controls in the sense that deviations have stronger and more immediate negative effects on economic growth. Market integration or globalization magnifies the effects of policies.

Implementation of structural adjustment programmes creates opportunities for more rapid growth, but it also increases the risk of low growth. This feature is probably more pronounced in many African countries than elsewhere, since they have weak governments that for various reasons are less likely to pursue growth-oriented policies. In addition, they are regularly exposed to serious external shocks, such as terms-of-trade changes and drought, requiring policy action that is often unpopular among the public.

This chapter is structured in the following way: First we discuss economic growth and its determinants in Africa in general, then the process of international economic integration in Africa is reviewed. Subsequently we analyse the political economy of adjustment in Africa, followed by an outlining of the prerequisites for successful integration into the world market. It is noted that increased exposure to international prices and returns on assets makes the economic equilibrium relations, the law of one price (LOP) and uncovered interest parity (UIP), relevant guiding lines for economic policy. The case of Zimbabwe is then presented, illustrating the arguments in the previous sections. It shows that lack of respect for the restrictions imposed by international markets may lead to an economic crisis with negative growth rates and a process away from globalization. The chapter ends with some concluding remarks.

Economic Growth in Africa

At the aggregate level one can decompose growth into a share that is due to factor accumulation and another share that is due to total factor productivity growth. The interesting question is, of course, what determines factor accumulation and productivity growth, and we will focus on that after looking at some growth decomposition results.

O'Connell and Ndulu (2000) have decomposed growth in a cross-section of countries and grouped the results into regions and periods. Table 1 shows that Africa has done worse than other regions on all counts, that is with regard to the contribution to growth from capital accumulation, human capital accumulation, and productivity growth. The situation has not improved in relative terms in the first half of the 1990s either, that is, a period in which structural adjustment measures were being implemented in Africa with varying degrees of commitment.

Table 1. Growth Accounting Decomposition by Region, 1960–1994

Region or half-decade	Number of countries	Observed growth	Contributions to growth of		
			Physical capital	Education	Residual
Growth decomposition by region 1960–1994					
SSA	21	0.41	0.61	0.23	-0.42
LAC	22	0.91	0.67	0.35	-0.11
SASI	4	2.33	1.17	0.3	0.86
EAP	9	3.86	2.2	0.5	1.15
MENAT	11	2.82	1.5	0.41	0.91
INDU	21	2.7	1.29	0.33	1.08
All countries	88	1.82	1.08	0.34	0.4
Deviation from sample means by region, 1960–1994					
SSA	21	-1.41	-0.48	-0.11	-0.82
LAC	22	-0.91	-0.42	0.02	-0.51
SASI	4	0.50	0.08	-0.03	0.46
EAP	9	2.04	1.12	0.17	0.75
MENAT	11	0.99	0.41	0.07	0.51
INDU	21	0.87	0.20	-0.01	0.68
All countries	88	0	0	0	0
Sub-Saharan Africa, deviations from half-decade full-sample means					
1960–64	21	-1.66	-0.53	-0.08	-1.05
1965–69	21	-1.47	-0.47	-0.10	-0.90
1970–74	21	-0.55	-0.24	-0.19	-0.13
1975–79	21	+1.97	-0.56	-0.20	-1.20
1980–84	21	-1.55	-0.50	-0.10	-0.95
1985-89	21	-0.24	-0.35	-0.07	-0.17
1990–94	21	-2.44	-0.70	-0.04	-1.71
All periods	21	-1.41	-0.48	-0.11	-0.82

Source: O'Connell and Ndulu, 2000, p. 29.
SSA – Sub-Saharan Africa, LAC – Latin America and the Caribbean, SASI – South Asia, EAP – East Asia and Pacific, MENAT – Middle East and North Africa, INDU – Industrialised countries

O'Connell and Ndulu then do a standard cross-country growth regression, which essentially confirms that Sub-Saharan Africa stands out negatively from the rest of the world. While individual policy variables seldom perform consistently across specifications, it is rare for a set of policy variables to be jointly insignificant in a growth regression. The results, reported in Table 2, can be seen to give an indication of the joint significance of the policy variables included.[1]

Table 2. Decomposition based on a pooled regression

Region	Deviation of actual growth from sample mean	Baseline variables	Contribution of:		
			Political instability	Policy	Residual
SSA	-1.14	-0.12	0.11	-1.05	-0.15
LAC	-0.93	-0.2	-0.1	-0.18	-0.46
SASI	0.68	1.59	-0.21	-1.17	0.57
EAP	2.35	1.48	0.07	0.65	0.14
MENAT	0.71	0.18	-0.03	0.04	0.56
INDU	0.18	-0.65	0.04	0.8	0.01

Source: O'Connell and Ndulu, 2000, p. 40.

In the past, African governments supported inefficient import-substituting activities. These activities operated behind high tariff walls, with preferential treatment being awarded to the import-substituting activities for getting scarce foreign exchange resources for importing machinery and inputs. This bias, along with the overvalued exchange rate, resulted in export not expanding as it could have. Trade reforms and policies aimed at reducing the anti-export bias ensure that resources are better allocated. The other way that trade policies can enhance growth is by helping the export sector to have access to technical knowledge from the world market. By integrating with global markets, firms in the export sector are also forced to be more competitive.

That distortions really have been extremely severe is indicated by a comparison done by O'Connell and Ndulu (2000, p. 26) who find that for the period 1970–1989 the share of investment in GDP at international prices in SSA was 10.1%, while its share at domestic prices was 18.9%. The numbers for industrialised countries at that time were 26.6% and 24.3%. This suggests that African investors were paying more than twice as much as their competitors in the industrial countries for investment goods. That by itself could explain a big part of the growth shortfall in Africa during this period.

---

1. The variables included in this specification are log of initial income, life expectancy, age dependency ratio, growth of potential labour force participation, terms of trade shocks, trading partner growth, landlocked, political instability, financial depth, inflation, black market premium, and government non-productive consumption/GDP, ratio of manufacturing trade to GDP, and fiscal deficit and grant/GDP.

Factor accumulation and productivity growth can be disaggregated further. Factor accumulation can occur because new agents enter or because existing agents accumulate more factors. Productivity growth may result from the more productive agents crowding out the less productive ones, or because some agents innovate and increase the productivity of their operations. By this categorization there are thus four dimensions of growth to consider.

One concern with regard to African economies noted by Collier and Gunning (1999b) is that neither in the case of farms nor firms do the more productive ones seem to grow faster than the less productive ones. This is a puzzle that it seems important to understand in our search for explanations of Africa's poor performance.

Factor accumulation in rural Africa over the last 50 years occurred mainly in labour and human capital, but to a very limited extent in physical capital. Of the major reasons for the low levels of investment the first is that the economic environment is very risky (Collier and Gunning, 1999a,b). Farmers have responded to this by diversification and by holding liquid assets to be able to smooth consumption. Secondly, land right systems have made rural investments unnecessarily illiquid. Thirdly, farmers are held back from undertaking large lucrative investments in a risky environment with poorly developed credit markets. They are instead locked into low-return, capital-extensive activities. Other reasons for this in the case of Africa are that movable wealth may attract violence, which may be a strong disincentive to accumulate in factors other than land. There is also often a high level of implicit taxation of successful individuals within the extended family system. In addition, rural investment is held back by the lack of social capital. There is a lack of marketable property rights and a multiplicity of social obligations as part of the rural insurance system.

Rural productivity growth can also be driven by the reallocation of activities from less productive to more productive farmers, but this is constrained by the imperfect land, credit and labour markets. Collier and Gunning (1999b) note that learning from others is confined to rather limited groups because rural households tend to have limited networks. Nor has learning-by-doing or innovations across the whole population been successful.

Collier and Gunning identify five major constraints on growth of urban firms in Africa, namely risk, lack of openness, lack of social capital, poor public services, and lack of financial depth. First, firms in Africa face high price risks, and this is particularly problematic when it is hard to reverse investment decisions. There are very limited markets for second-hand capital or for firms as a going concern. Local suppliers to the firm are often unreliable which means that firms tend to carry large stocks of inventories. Firms also enter into state-contingent contracts.

Lack of openness is also a major constraint on investment in Africa. Foreign exchange controls made some investments hard to undertake, and overvalued exchange rates did, at least earlier, often make a mockery of economic calculations of economic returns on investments. Some investments made in highly distorted settings, such as Tanzania, turned out to have no economic value at all once the economy was liberalised and world market prices arrived. The liberalization has also implied increased competition and many firms do actually complain about this. The movement from the old environment to a new competitive one is not painless, and in for example Zambia many of the old manufacturing industries were not viable in the new open environment but went bankrupt. Now the survivors are expanding, however, and some non-traditional exporters are also successful in export markets. However, so far these have mainly had to be found within the region. Export to the North, which is the real challenge, is still stagnant (Bigsten, Mkenda, 2001).

It is not self-evident that manufacturing production will expand when African economies liberalize. There are several authors, Adrian Wood[1] in particular, who argue that this is not where African economies in general have their comparative advantages because of their abundance of natural resources and lack of human capital. Others argue that the problem is related to the high cost of transactions, energy, and other inputs in manufacturing that are intensive. The first view suggests that trade reform would kill off the major part of African manufacturing, and that this is just as well since it is intrinsically uncompetitive. The second thesis suggests instead that reforms of trade policy and service delivery would create an environment where African manufacturing could grow.

There is a lack of social capital, which could help contract enforcement, which is a big problem in the risky environment of Africa. African courts are often unreliable, slow and open to political influence. The legal process is slow and the outcomes are uncertain. In an environment where there are essentially no credit rating institutions businessmen have to rely on kin-groups. The extent and character of the kin-group then determines what can be achieved in business. In Kenya, for instance, the Asian ethnic minority has an advantage over the African owned manufacturing industry since they can exploit their relatively well-developed network of business associates (Bigsten, Kimuyu, Lundvall, 2000).

The traditional social structures or social capital of Africa developed in response to the need to deal with the difficult economic conditions that prevailed. The family, the village or some kin-group helped reduce problems of adverse selection and moral hazards in rural areas. Apart from the insurance function they also helped with inter-generational transfers and the management of common resources. The traditional societies managed to devise coping mechanisms for the traditional environment, but these also came to constitute a break in investment and specialization.

---

1. See for example Wood (1994), Wood and Berge (1997), Wood and Mayer (1999).

Poor infrastructure is a severe constraint on growth in African manufacturing.[1] This is of course related to the poor functioning in general of the public sector and this is one of the areas in which structural adjustment measures have found it hardest to bring about improvements.

The shallowness of financial markets is a hindrance to growth, although the problem of lack of finance is sometimes exaggerated. Many businessmen tend to believe that they will do fine if they just get credit, while the main constraint on their development is rather poor productivity.

We may conclude that economic life in Africa is risky and the effect of this on growth is compounded by poor contract enforcement mechanisms, poor infrastructure and the uncertainty about the macroeconomic environment.

Is Africa Integrating with the Global Economy?

There are two schools of thought on the development of international economic integration in Africa during recent decades. The first one argues that Africa has not benefited from globalization because it has not globallized. The declining share of Africa in world trade is taken as an indication of this. This view suggests that it is crucial to Africa's economic recovery that it pursues export promotion policies to open up further (World Bank, 2000, Sachs, 2000). There are many studies that suggest that international economic integration is beneficial for growth (see the survey by Collier and Gunning, 1999a). The second school suggests that Africa did take advantage of trading opportunities in accordance with its income and level of development. This view suggests that the causality runs from growth and productivity to trade, and that the policy focus needs to be on the broader range of issues determining productivity.

First, it is clear that Africa's share in world export fell from 3.5% in 1970 to 1.5% in 1997, and its share in world imports fell from 4.5% to 1.5% during the same period. That Africa's share of world trade has declined is thus abundantly clear. The next question that one may pose is whether its current share is atypical relative to some benchmark. Studies that have approached this issue have done it in different ways, but generally they have used gravity models. Foroutan and Pritchett (1993) compared Africa with other third world countries and concluded that the intra-Africa trade pattern is not atypical and that distances impose similar restrictions as in other similar regions. Coe and Hoffmaister (1997) investigated North-South trade and found that in 1970 Africa "overtraded" with the North, while in the 1990s its trade flows were not different from those of comparable non-African countries. Rodrik (1999) just looked at aggregate trade and found that Africa's total trade is not atypical after controlling for income, size, and distance to the world markets.

---

1. See Bigsten and Kimuyu (2001) for evidence on Kenya.

A recent study by Subramanian and Tamirisa (2001) shows that over the period 1980–1997 Anglophone African trade grew by 2.1% per year, while Francophone trade only grew by 1.6% per year. For the Anglophone countries trade within the region grew by 9.4% per year and trade with the South by 8.9% per year. Trade with the North, however, only grew by 0.9% per year. Francophone trade with the South grew rapidly, but from a very low base.

Francophone Africa undertrades in total, both with the North and with the South. It is only within the group itself that it does not undertrade. The trend is negative, that is Francophone Africa becomes less and less economically intregrated with the rest of the world. While its global trade was about normal in 1980, it was 52% below average in 1997. The trade with the North declined from normal to 75% below average. This is an amazing and alarming decline. Since much of technology transfer comes via trade (Coe, Helpman, Hoffmaister, 1997) this may have serious implications for the ability of the Francophone countries to catch up with the faster growing regions.

The situation for the Anglophone countries is better. In 1997 it was still not significantly different from average, although also here there was a negative (although not significant) trend in its degree of export orientation. Anglophone countries traded more than average within the group itself, while trade with the South and non-Lomé industrial countries were typical.

The benchmark so far has been all international trade, but it may be argued that it would be more reasonable to compare with other developing countries. This is also done by Subramanian and Tamirisa (2001), and the analysis shows that even relative to other developing countries Africa under-performs. And even more distressingly, Africa has gradually become less economically integrated with the rest of the world, while the rest of the developing world has been rapidly integrating. The conclusion from the study is that there is a marginalization process. Africa has not benefited from globalization because it has not globalized in the first place. Both Francophone and Anglophone Africa have seen a negative trend in export orientation relative to the level predicted given their economic characteristics, but the level for Anglophone Africa is still average, while it is much below average for Francophone Africa.

Moreover, it is particularly in trade with the North that Africa has been lagging behind, and this is serious since it is via this trade that many of the expected benefits of globalization would come. The results do not depend on the concentration on commodity exports, and the situation looks even more acute when one notices that the rest of the developing world has integrated at a rapid pace with the rest of the world including the North. Africa needs to develop its trading system, introduce measures that facilitate export diversification as well as measures that increase productivity and competitiveness.

Whichever way one looks at the debate on the causal relationship between trade and growth it is hard to envisage rapid growth without trade expansion in Africa. Opening up is essential for such a trade expansion to take place, and we would argue that it is a necessary condition for rapid growth. However, is it sufficient? The rest of the chapter discusses the problems of pursuing a policy aimed at growth in a more open and internationally integrated setting, and the reasons why things may go wrong.

The Political Economy of Adjustment in Africa

We believe that the opening up of African economies in most cases has acted as a restraint on the behaviour of economic policy makers. Some countries like Uganda have done very well. However, many leaders of other countries, and the example we have chosen is Zimbabwe, still act as if they are unaware of the constraints or, which may be more likely, act in accordance with more fundamental incentives. We will discuss the basis for this argument here.

Successful market economies have an underpinning of sound institutions. Rodrik (2000) provides the following list:

a) The first is secure *property rights*. North and Thomas (1973) and North and Wein-gast (1989) show that the establishment of secure and stable property rights was a key factor behind the development of western economies. It is not self-evident, however, that the property rights have to look exactly the same everywhere. Rodrik actually prefers the term control rights, which allows for different forms of rights. These are upheld by a combination of legislation, private enforcement, and customs.

b) It has also been shown that markets do not function well when participants are involved in fraud and anti-competitive behaviour. These economies need a set of *regulatory institutions* that regulate the conduct in goods, services, labour, asset and financial markets.

c) Economies also need to have fiscal and monetary institutions for macroeconomic stabilization.

d) Rodrik also argues that economies need *institutions for social insurance*. In traditional economies this was handled by family and village linkages and support systems, which tend to weaken once a modernization of the economy takes place. Such programmes could be of the traditional transfer type like in Western welfare societies, but they can also take other forms. Social insurance is important since it legitimises the market economy and provides social stability and social cohesion. Economic insecurity may breed backlashes to reforms, and the control of it may therefore have high payoffs by making much needed reforms politically feasible.

e) Societies should also have some *institutions for conflict management*. Many countries in Africa are, for example, ethnically diverse, and they need some mechanisms to settle disputes. Social conflicts divert resources from productive activities and create uncertainty with negative effects on economic activity. There may be coordination failures in which social factions fail to coordinate on outcomes that would be mutually beneficial. Developed societies have institutions that reduce the likelihood of such failures. Institutions of this nature listed by Rodrik (2000, p. 13) are "the rule of law, a high-quality judiciary, representative political institutions, free elections, independent trade unions, social partnerships, institutionalised representation of minority groups and social insurance".

So what can we say about these institutions in the context of Africa? One fundamental part of the institutional structure is the state. It is more in a way a meta-institution that determines or influences the ways in which a whole range of institutions in the economy works. Africa's peculiar history and its specific conditions may help explain why the African state works in a certain way and why policies are formulated in a special way. It is therefore important to investigate in some detail how the state works and how globalization impulses are transmitted through it.

The Emergence of the African State

The African states of today emerged out of the colonial system in the early 1960s. It seems plausible to assume that the character of the state today reflects this history. Engelbert (2000) argues that the root cause of poor African growth is to be found in policymaking, and that it is constrained by the lack of continuity of the African state from the colonial to the post-colonial era. This constrains the choices open to African governments. "Specifically, the relative power payoffs of developmental policies for political elites are lower in countries where the state was arbitrarily imposed over pre-existing institutions leading them to resort instead to redistributive policies that retard or hinder growth" (Engelbert, 2000, p. 1822). Africa has a large concentration of states with little or no embeddedness into pre-colonial institutions and pre-existing norms of political authority. This makes the economic performance weaker according to Engelbert.

Africa has the highest concentration of states where the process of state creation was exogenous to the society and where the leadership or elite inherited the state rather than shaped it. The new rulers therefore had little power and had to deal with groups with competing loyalties. The citizens came to view the African state not so much as an outcome of a social contract, an instrument of collective action, or an instrument for reduction of transaction costs, based on common ideological convictions, but as an alien institution. They did not agree about the rules of the political game. Opposition focused not so much on policies as on the government itself. Because of this, African politics display high instability with constitutional deadlocks and military coups, secession attempts and civil wars.

For the ruling elite, power is thus fragile. The lack of state legitimacy has limited policy options. It is hard to pursue development policies when bureaucrats are not loyal to the state and private agents distrust it. In such a setting it is not surprising that the governments try to preserve their power base by neo-patrimonial measures. The state relies on the creation and maintenance of rents such as those derived from trade restrictions, and a preference for distributive over long-term investments. Neo-patrimonial policies lead to widespread distortions in market mechanisms in order to allocate resources according to political rather than economic criteria.

The relative payoffs of developmental versus neo-patrimonial policies depend on state legitimacy. In legitimate states, institutions and rules do not face the challenges of pre-existing loci of power and are therefore able to use the state apparatus to implement development policies, which further enhances their legitimacy over time in a virtuous circle of capacity and development.

This analysis suggests that underlying the problems of Africa is a crisis of governance. African leaders do not primarily choose bad policies because they do not know any better. The historical circumstances determine the relative returns in terms of power of different strategies.

The Redistributive State, Ethnicity and Conflicts in Africa

Many have argued that the ethnic diversity of Africa breeds political conflicts or civil wars that reduce economic growth. It is also clear that ethnic diversity is correlated with slow economic growth (Easterly and Levine, 1997). What one may ask is whether this is the case irrespective of the form of government. Collier (2000) sets up a median voter type of model and uses it to investigate whether there is a difference in terms of impact depending on whether the government is democratic or dictatorial. His results suggest that ethnic diversity is only detrimental to growth in societies where there are limited political rights, while democratic societies are generally able to handle the potential conflicts without generating negative growth effects. A recent study by Easterly (forthcoming) extends the analysis further. He runs a set of growth regressions with an institutional quality variable, and he also interacts this with ethnolinguistic fractionalization. His main result is that if institutions are of very high quality, then the ethnic diversity does not harm growth prospects. He tests this result against a result from Collier, which suggests that democracy has this effect. Easterly however, finds that institutions knock out democracy, and suggests that it is the institutional quality variable that matters in this context.

Azam (2001) sees the problem of state formation in Africa as a transition process that starts from a situation with ethnic division. He argues that ethnic capital provides many of the services that have been taken over by the modern state in rich countries such as security, education, and rules of behaviour. Most African states are as yet not able to deliver these services adequately. Therefore they have to go through a phase of federation of ethnic groups before they can provide a credible substitute to ethnic capital. The existing system of redistribution within and among groups is a key to creating the solidarity links between them, and a breakdown in this system may lead to political violence or civil war.

The state and the ethnic groups are connected through the participation of ethnic elites in the state. Ethnic groups or in-groups invest collectively in their ablest members to migrate to the cities to become involved in the urban elite. This is a means to ensure political participation of the group. In the peaceful African countries a system of incursion of the educated members of various ethnic groups into different institutions has evolved, whereby the state buys loyalty from the groups through its educated urban "delegates". The maintenance of peace is one of the prime tasks of the state in Africa, but ethnically dominated governments have often neglected this. The ethnic groups are normally the basis for a rebellion as the many links that exist among the members provide an efficient way of overcoming the free-rider problem involved in organising an uprising.

In the typical African state the political elite is composed of people from different ethnic groups, who play the part of delegates from their group. People are there to receive high salaries or incomes that can be the basis for remittances back to their kin, but they may also collude in taxing the rural constituency. Many distortions in African policy making have their roots here. Thus, the urban elites may extract more from the rural areas than they remit back. But, notes Azam, this system is also instrumental in creating a new solidarity network that can help push ethnic links into the background.

The African state according to Azam is thus a means of federating different ethnic groups via a coalition of their elites, and it thus entails two interlinked redistribution systems. The first is a system of transfers within ethnic groups, whereby the urban elite remits money back to the village (regularly or when there is a shock). The second system is one with redistribution between ethnic groups, through the elite or via the budget. When the benefits of public expenditures are widely distributed the delegates of the ethnic groups can obtain renewed support from their backers. Azam's model is thus a redistribution-based model of the state.

The state buys loyalty from its social base via remittances from its urban workers or via the provision of public services. Insurgencies occur when some group becomes excluded from the sharing of the government resources. Insurgencies are generally led by the most educated of an ethnic group (Clapham, 1998), and they buy loyalty from their followers by securing resources for and redistributing them to the group. The likelihood that a group gets excluded is particularly high when the resources of the state are based on mineral resources. Collier and Hoeffler (1999) show that the share of minerals in exports is a significant variable in the explanation of civil wars.Azam thus argues that civil conflicts occur when the government is unable to deliver the kind of public expenditure that the people want with a strong redistributive element, such as education and health. He shows in a model that a government that is able to credibly commit to its announced public expenditure mix will resort more to redistributive expenditures and less to repression, than a government that can renege on its promises, once the potential opponents have reduced their involvement in the rebellion. Weak governments imply a repression bias, while strong governments will rely more on redistribution.

The policy problem for the African state is to substitute state-provided services for ethnic capital, starting from a situation with strong endowments of ethnic capital. The aim of the benevolent state during the transition should be to federate the different ethnic groups, and not to destroy their role. One tool is the provision of public goods with a strong redistributive content such as education and health care or the payment of high wages and salaries that then can be redistributed privately.

Why Ineffective Policy?

Policy making depends on the interaction between interest groups in different ways. In Africa there is extensive corruption and lack of effective control of mismanagement, and the interaction between politics and ethnic rivalries makes it hard to establish long-term stable and undistorted strategies (Bigsten and Moene, 1996). It may also be argued that apart from the ethnic dimension, the economic structure tends to influence political outcomes. For example, standard trade theory suggests that a country should optimally adjust its economy according to its comparative advantages. However, the comparative advantages may imply a policy that is counter to what is politically desirable. For example, if a country is land (or natural resources) abundant it may be inappropriate to let the wages of labour increase too fast, while we know that higher urban wages have been politically desirable in Africa (Bigsten and Kayizzi-Mugerwa, 2000).

So why are there no effective forces that can guarantee good governance? There is obviously a lack of democratic control also in the countries that have been democratised. The government in power often tends to look to the interests of its core supporters rather than the welfare of the country as a whole. The external pressure for democratic change has also been weak until recently, but it is possible that the economic reform programmes have to some extent contributed to political openness. It has been argued that what is lacking are agents of restraint that can force governments to behave responsibly and to introduce sensible economic policies and then to stay on track. The increased openness, and debate, in most African countries may in the longer term contribute to a change in this direction, but so far one cannot say that there has in general been a major change in government behaviour. Therefore much remains to be done before the political process can produce effective government and policy making.

What is Required for *Successful* Integration?

In African economies, structural adjustment programmes have been the major component of the globalization process. Standard programme packages have included trade liberalization, de-regulation of domestic markets and privatization, measures to achieve a realistic exchange rate, reduced budget deficits, tax reforms, restrictive monetary policy, and public sector reform. These measures were meant to make the countries' allocation of resources more economically rational. At the same time as the reforms have "got the prices right", they have also implied that the countries have become more sensitive to the actions of economic agents, domestic and foreign. One could presume that the structural adjustment packages would serve as disciplining devices forcing policy makers to exercise caution and not to suggest policies that depart from the new market economy path. In general, this should thus push countries towards increased macroeconomic stability and towards a better growth performance; if the policy makers stray from the narrow path, the punishment from the market is more severe than under the old control regime. For instance, even loose statements may have large effects on the foreign currency markets, which will then affect the fortunes of the economy. And when policies à la Mugabe are put in place, the economic consequences are now much more severe than they would have been under the old system.

A major aspect of the opening up of an economy and the attempt to integrate it with the world market is increased exposure to international prices and returns on assets. This exposure can be captured by two simple economic equilibrium relations that are expected to hold in well-integrated markets, the law of one price (LOP) and uncovered interest parity (UIP). The former implies that similar goods should have similar prices even if they are produced and sold in different countries. If prices diverge, moving the goods from the low price country to the high price one can make profits. The latter relationship states that the expected return on a financial asset should be approximately the same in the two countries. Otherwise people will move their assets to the one with the highest expected return. The two relationships can be written as:

$$P_k \approx E * P_k^* \qquad LOP$$

$$i \approx i^* + \Delta E^{\exp} \qquad UIP$$

"where P_k is the price of the good k, E is the exchange rate, $\Delta E^{\exp}$ is the expected change of the exchange rate, i is the return on financial assets, and an asterisk indicates world prices or interest rates".

In practice LOP and UIP do not hold exactly even when markets are well integrated; there are transportation costs, limited information, differences in risks, etc. In spite of this, the two relationships do restrict movements of prices, interest rates and the exchange rate because there are limits on how far away they can be from the equilibrium conditions values, particularly in small open countries.

Before structural adjustment there were very weak or no forces maintaining LOP and UIP in most Sub-Saharan African countries. Domestic prices could differ considerably from international prices of similar goods. The major reasons were the restrictions on international trade in the form of import quotas and tariffs, bans on exports, and limited access to foreign currency. It was simply harder to make profits by exploiting price differences in such an environment than in a country with free trade. Moreover, interest parity did not hold because domestic interest rates were set administratively at low levels, the domestic currency was not convertible, and the authorities controlled capital flows in and out of the country.

The efficiency of the system of controls on international transactions varied between countries. In many countries smuggling was common, there were thriving parallel markets for foreign exchange and goods, and companies used transfer pricing to keep foreign exchange outside the home country. Nevertheless, substantial deviations from LOP and UIP were common. These are likely to have had negative effects on the economic performance. However, in the controlled economy environment the negative effects were often not obvious to policymakers or people in general because they were smaller than in open economies, and appeared slowly over time. Hence, policymakers did not bother too much about LOP and UIP.

Structural adjustment considerably increased the potential for international arbitrage. Evidence of this is the removal of many restrictions on international trade, the decrease in importance, or disappearance, of parallel markets for foreign exchange and the creation of official foreign exchange markets, and the increase in capital flows. There is thus reason to believe that in Sub-Saharan countries LOP and UIP have become important equilibrium relationships to which the authorities must pay attention, and they thus restrict the policy choices of the government considerably. Moreover, external shocks, such as drought or changes in export prices, often require government action to facilitate the adjustment, since shocks can generate large deviations from equilibrium in the short run.

Policy making in a country that is becoming integrated in the global economy is thus very different from that in a controlled economy. For example, an expected decline of exports, or a statement by leading politicians, can generate large capital outflows and a drop in the value of the local currency. The increase in the exchange rate can then rapidly be transmitted into higher domestic prices of basic commodities. Hence, to benefit from globalization policymakers have to accept the discipline imposed by the LOP and UIP restrictions. On the other hand, if they do not, the negative consequences are far more serious than before structural adjustment. Below we describe the case of Zimbabwe to illustrate the consequences of policymaking that is in sharp conflict with LOP and UIP.

The Case of Zimbabwe

Zimbabwe's structural adjustment programme was started late in 1990 and was planned to last until 1995. In general the programme was implemented according to plan, and in some respects even faster than that. However, there were repeated failures to meet the targets for the budget deficit. Together with a combination of policy mistakes and external shocks, the accumulation of public debt that resulted from the budget deficits, set off a crisis late in 1997 that within a few years led to a national disaster. Without this development, it is likely that the popularity of the government would have been much greater today and that many of the disastrous events that have taken place during recent years could have been avoided. Below follows a brief account of the developments that led to the current crisis. It highlights that care must be exercised by the authorities because of the constraints imposed by LOP and UIP and that adequate policy responses to external shocks are important for the maintenance of a high level of economic growth.

Although the IMF declared Zimbabwe off-track at the end of 1995 and several donors withheld disbursements of foreign aid, the economy grew by 7.3% in 1996 and the prospects for the future looked good. The losses of the public enterprises had been reduced significantly and the budget deficit as a ratio to GDP was declining. The improvement in fiscal policies and the budget presented for 1997/98 persuaded the World Bank that the economy was on the right track again, and it decided to release the second tranche of the second structural adjustment credit in mid-1997. However, just before the agreement was to be signed President Mugabe announced that more than Z$4 billion (3% of GDP) had been promised to war veterans in compenzation and pensions. This unexpected and unplanned increase in public expenditures made it impossible for the World Bank to release the money.

In conjunction with the failure to reach an agreement with the World Bank, three other important events took place. First, during late 1996 and early 1997 there were adverse developments in export volumes and prices, and a rapid increase in imports. This led to a large trade deficit and downward pressure on the exchange rate. By defending the value of the currency, the authorities reduced foreign reserves sharply. Second, in an attempt to boost its popularity among the public after the agreement over compenzation to the war veterans, the government announced that close to 1,500, out of 4,000, mainly white-owned commercial farms would be nationalised during 1998. This announcement was made without clarifying how the nationalization would be financed or to what extent farmers would receive compenzation for their property. Third, because of el Niño, fears were created about a serious drought in 1998, which would raise food prices and reduce export income.

All this contributed to a severe currency crisis in November 1997 when the Zimbabwe dollar plummeted. To curb the crisis, the Reserve Bank ordered all companies to liquidate their foreign currency accounts, and tightened up monetary policy.

Shortly after the government announced tax increases to finance the war veterans' compenzation. But the party conference held a few days later unanimously rejected this measure, and a wave of strikes hit the country. Over the following year the crisis deepened as basic food prices rose rapidly, and yet another currency crisis took place reducing the value of the Zimbabwe dollar by 50% against the US dollar. On top of all this Zimbabwe entered the war in the Democratic Republic of Congo.

These events highlight the increased interaction between politics and the economy; liberalization has created a situation where government policies are evaluated by the market in a way that makes costs and benefits much more visible to the public than in the old regime. Earlier, an event like the announcement of the badly planned land redistribution would not have led to any visible reaction at a macro-level, at least not in the short run. However, in a liberalised environment where international trade is free and there are markets for foreign exchange and agricultural commodities, the response is immediate. This was amply illustrated by the rapid rise in prices of basic commodities during 1998 when government policies generated expectations about a sharp reduction in future supply of agricultural products.

One important change in policy that disrupted the arbitrage conditions was the fixing of the exchange rate by government decree. The purpose was to reduce inflation in general and stabilize food prices in particular. But since there was no progress in reducing the budget deficit, which was the fundamental driving force behind the price increases, domestic inflation continued to be high. As a result the real exchange rate appreciated, and at the end of 1999 foreign exchange shortages started to appear.

The evolution of the nominal exchange rate, measured in Zimbabwe dollars per US dollar, is depicted in the upper panel of Figure 1 for the period 1980–2002. During the 1980s there was a slow and steady increase in the exchange rate. This should be contrasted with the rapid drop in the value of the Zimbabwe dollar after the initialization of the structural adjustment programme in 1991. There were several prolonged periods of stable exchange rates that ended with a major devaluation; the period after 1997 is particularly illuminating since the size of devaluations clearly shows that the fixed exchange rate policy was unsustainable.

The lower panel of Figure 1 shows the development of the real exchange rate. Clearly, PPP did not hold over the period 1980–2002, although it might have held for a period after 1992. Nevertheless, comparing the real and nominal exchange rate reveals that relative prices account for most of the variation in the latter; rapid inflation in Zimbabwe is the major explanation for the decline in the value of its currency. Figure 1 also shows that the trade liberalization of the beginning of the 1990s generated a real depreciation. The consequence of the policy of fixing the exchange rate is evident from the huge swings in the real exchange rate, particularly from 1998. It is not hard to imagine the difficulties that economic agents face with such

Figure 1. Upper panel: the Zimbabwe - US dollar exchange rate. Lower panel: the real exchange rate defined as the Zimbabwe – US dollar exchange rate times the US wholesale price index divided by Zimbabwe's consumer price index (1990:1 = 1).

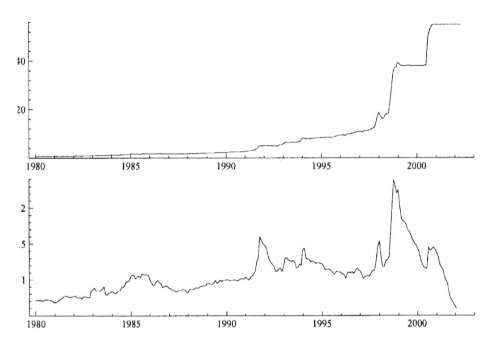

large changes in relative prices. Towards the end of the 1990s there is rapid growth in parallel markets due to rationing of goods and foreign currency, and the values of the real exchange rate presented become less relevant. Already by the end of 2001, the parallel exchange rate passed 350 Zimbabwe dollars to one US dollar, while the official exchange rate remained at 55 dollars. Furthermore, the official consumer price index successively became a less representative measure of the changes in the price level as trade moved to the informal markets.

Another policy response that created huge disequilibria is revealed by Figure 2, which compares the real Treasury bill rate in Zimbabwe and the real three-month Eurodollar rate for the period 1990–2002. They provide information similar to the UIP but are easier to interpret. During the 1980s real interest rates in Zimbabwe were in general negative and there was no relation to international interest rates; restrictions on foreign exchange and financial markets and controls on capital flows made it almost impossible to exploit differences in returns. Liberalization of the foreign exchange and financial markets led to increases in interest rates and from the beginning of 1993 until 1996 returns to investment were high in Zimbabwe leading to large capital inflows. However, during the late 1990s macroeconomic instability in combination with changes in monetary policy first led to a drop in the real interest rate to about 0%, and then to a sharp increase to over 20%. The increase in real inter-

Figure 2. The real Treasury bill rate in Zimbabwe (——) and the real three-month Eurodollar rate (——)

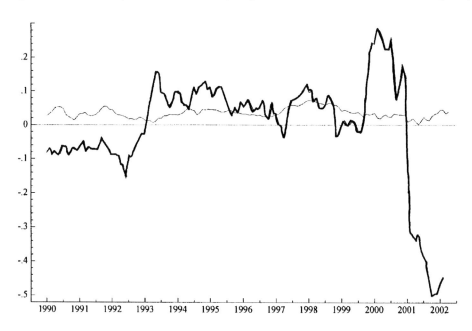

est rates contributed to ballooning interest rate payments on the government's domestic debt. As a reaction, the government tried to reduce interest payment by issuing long-term bonds instead of Treasury bills. As a result interest rates on Treasury bills dropped to less than 10% and real interest rates declined to less than -30%. Since financing the debt by issuing long-term bonds failed, a process of monetization of the debt started, leading to even higher inflation. In 2003 inflation reached 400%.

Yet another reaction of the government was to re-introduce price controls on some basic commodities to calm down public opinion. It might appear to be socially preferable to artificially keep prices of basic consumer goods below world prices. Although such a policy can have beneficial effects in the short run, i.e. for a couple of months, it is not a good strategy when used over several years. With low prices, exports of goods with controlled prices become profitable for some economic agents but not for Zimbabwe as a country. For example, the government-run Grain Marketing Board appears to have exported maize grain to make profits during 1998 (see Muchero 1998), creating shortages and stimulating price increases in the domestic market for maize meal. Moreover, large amounts of maize (meal) were probably exported illegally to neighbouring countries; there is at least evidence that tons of maize meal were carried across Victoria Bridge to Zambia, before the authorities stopped the trade. After that people switched to trading in bread. Table 3 shows the evolution of different prices for maize over the period 1990 to 1998. The possibilities for making profits by exporting during 1998 are obvious.

Another problem with the price controls is that they are selective; for instance, producer prices of maize and maize meal prices are controlled but prices on inputs used in maize production, such as fertilisers, pesticides, and seeds are influenced by world prices. Hence, unless productivity increases, profits from maize production will decline as world prices rise, and both commercial and communal farmers shift to other crops.

Table 3. International Maize Prices (US dollars per tonne)

	1990	1991	1992	1993	1994	1995	1996	1997	1998
Import price	224.1	208.8	197.0	197.2	628.8	310.2	203.2	236.9	202.5
Export price	146.8	108.7	359.9	145.5	114.7	117.1	151.1	125.4	111.6
World price	95.3	91.3	90.6	89.0	94.5	102.8	149.2	103.9	86.6
Producer price	81.7	45.0	48.6	77.0	108.0	99.0	94.5	60.0	36.0

Note: The export and import prices were taken from FAO's database. They were calculated by dividing the values of the exports and imports by their respective quantities. The world price is the Chicago Board of Trade price for yellow maize, taken from the IFS database. Producer prices are from the GMB.

One of the prices that the government did not relinquish its control over was the price of fuel. The evolution of world fuel prices in Zimbabwe dollars and domestic prices are depicted in Figure 3. Both price series are set to unity in 1990, highlighting the slow adjustment of domestic prices between 1995 and the end of 2000. During

Figure 3. Indexes for the world price of petrol measured in Zimbabwe dollars (——) and the domestic petrol price (——). The value in 1990:1 is set to unity

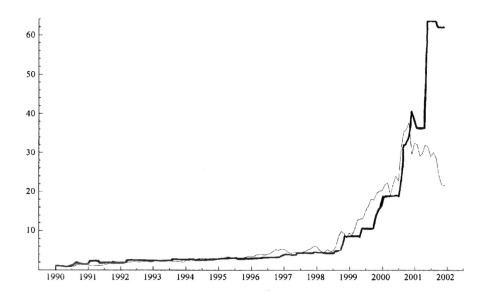

the late 1990s shortages of foreign exchange created shortages of fuel, and this probably accounts for the dramatic increase in domestic prices in 2000. One consequence of keeping an artificially low price was higher consumption of energy than otherwise. This was of course one of the reasons for the price policy, but it contributed to the shortages of foreign exchange. However, there were other side effects. Since government kept local prices low when world prices, in domestic currency, increased, the parastatal responsible for importing fuel, NOCZIM, made large operating losses. During some periods it was selling fuel at a lower price than what it paid for it. Another side effect was that a great of deal re-exporting of fuel took place. It is hard to quantify its importance, but it is well known some South African trailers were equipped with extra tanks, so they could go to Zimbabwe to buy cheap petrol.

To conclude, it is evident that the Zimbabwean government has paid little attention to the restrictions imposed on policy making by the markets. The most fundamental mistake was probably to allow the domestic debt to get out of hand. Although President Mugabe was aware of the debt problem he did not seem to understand its consequences. This is evident from the following comment he made soon after giving in to the war veterans "Have you ever heard of a country that collapsed because of borrowing?" (Meredith 2002, p. 138). In fact, the direct effects have been devastating, and in combination with the political problems that ensued they have led to a national disaster. GDP growth turned negative in 1999 and by 2002 the economy had contracted by about 30%, and there are widespread shortages of food and other goods. Moreover, inflation, measured with the consumer price index, passed 400% in 2003, and it is likely to be much higher if goods in informal markets are considered. Hence, without a combined effort of the government and the international community to solve the debt problem and stabilise prices further deterioration of the economy can be expected.

Conclusions

So what is the way forward? Globalization is not a panacea for development! It can help, but for the effects in terms of economic growth of opening-up to be substantial other aspects of the economy also have to be in order. The macroeconomic policies must be right as well as the institutions supporting the economy. Excessive corruption, poor policies or poorly implemented policies will negate the effect of attempts to open up and integrate in the world economy. Will opening-up also help the system to reform itself in more domestic dimensions? This is hard to prove one way or the other, but it does not seem unreasonable to believe that a more open environment will make it harder to be corrupt and to pursue counter-productive policies.

Hopefully the recent experience of Zimbabwe will provide a good example of the devastating effects of carrying out policies that ignore market mechanisms. Such policies could be implemented with less obvious negative effects before structural adjustment, that is when domestic markets were much less integrated into the world economy. However, economic success in a globalized world is dependent on policies that respect the constraints imposed by markets.

References

Azam, J-P. (2001), *The Redistributive Role of the State*. Working Paper No 2001.3, Centre for the Study of African Economies. Oxford: Oxford University.

Bigsten, A. (2002), "Can Africa Catch Up?", *World Economics* 3(2).

Bigsten, A. and S. Kayizzi-Mugerwa (2000), "The Political Economy of Policy Failure in Zambia", forthcoming in Lundahl, M., Wyzan, M.L. (eds.) *The Political Economy of Policy Reform Failure*. London: Routledge.

Bigsten, A. and P. Kimuyu (eds.) (2001), *Structure and Performance of Manufacturing in Kenya*. London: Palgrave.

Bigsten, A., P. Kimuyu and K. Lundvall (2000), "Informality, Ethnicity and Productivity. Evidence from Small Manufacturers in Kenya", Working Paper in Economics no 27, Department of Economics, Göteborg University.

Bigsten, A. and K-O. Moene (1996), "Growth and Rent Dissipation: The Case of Kenya , *Journal of African Economies,* 5(2).

Bigsten, A. and B. Mkenda (2001), "Impacts of Trade Liberalisation in Zambia". Mimeo, Göteborg University.

Clapham, C. (ed.) (1998), *African Guerrillas.* Oxford: James Currey.

Coe, D., E. Helpman and A. Hoffmaister (1997), "North–South R&D Spillovers", *Economic Journal* 107(1).

Coe, D. and A. Hoffmaister(1999), "North–South Trade: Is Africa Unusual*?", Journal of African Economies* 8(2).

Collier, P. (2000), "Ethnicity, Politics and Economic Performance", *Economics and Politics* 12(3).

Collier, P. and J. Gunning (1999a), "Explaining African Economic Performance", *Journal of Economic Literature* 37(1).

Collier, P. and J. Gunning (1999b), "The Microeconomics of African Growth, 1950–2000". Mimeo, AERC, Nairobi.

Collier, P. and A. Hoeffler (1999), "Justice-Seeking and Loot-Seeking in Civil War". Mimeo, World Bank, Washington DC.

Easterly, W. (2001), "Can Institutions Resolve Ethnic Conflict?", *Economic Development and Cultural Change* 49(4).

Easterly, W. and R. Levine (1997), "Africa's Growth Tragedy", *Quarterly Journal of Economics* 112(4).

Engelbert, P. (2000), "Solving the Mystery of the AFRICA Dummy", *World Development* 28(10).

Foroutan, F. and L. Pritchett (1993), "Intra-Sub-Saharan African Trade: Is It Too Little?", *Journal of African Economies 2(1).*

Melchior, A., K. Telle and H. Wiig (2000), *Globalization and Inequality: World Income Distribution and Living Standards, 1960–1998.* Oslo: Norwegian Ministry of Foreign Affairs.

Meredith, M. (2002) *Mugabe.* Oxford: Public Affairs Ltd.

Muchero, M. (1998) "The Role of GMB in Between These Interests" in *Staple Food and Producer Prices: Whereto Do They Go?*. Seminar Proceedings (17). Harare: Friedrich-Ebert-Stiftung, Economic Advisory Project.

North, D.C. and R. Thomas (1973), *The Rise of the Western World: A New Economic History.* Cambridge: Cambridge University Press.

North, D.C. and B. Weingast (1989), "Constitutions and Commitment: The Evolution of Institutions Governing Public Choice in Seventeenth Century England", *Journal of Economic History 49(4)*.

O'Connell, S. and B.J. Ndulu (2000), "Africa's Growth Experience: A Focus on Sources of Growth". Mimeo, AERC, Nairobi.

Rodrik, D. (1999), *Making Openness Work.* London: Overseas Development Institute.

Rodrik, D. (2000), "Institutions for High-Quality Growth: What They Are and How They Acquire Them", NBER Working Paper No 7540, Cambridge Mass..

Sachs, J. (2000), "Tropical Underdevelopment", paper presented at the Economic History Association's 69th Annual Meeting.

Subramanian, A. and N. Tamirisa (2001), "Africa's Trade Revisited", IMF Working Paper WP/01/33, Washington DC.

Wood, A. (1994), *North–South Trade. Employment and Inequality.* Oxford: Clarendon Press.

Wood, A. and K. Berge (1997), "Exporting Manufactures: Human Resources, Natural Resources and Trade Policy", *Journal of Development Studies* 34(1).

Wood, A. and J. Mayer (1999), "Africa's Export Structure in a Comparative Perspective". Mimeo, IDS, University of Sussex.

World Bank (2000), *Can Africa Claim the 21st Century?,* Washington DC.

4. Support for Economic Reform? Popular Attitudes in Southern Africa

Michael Bratton and Robert Mattes[1]

Introduction

We live in an era of shrinking states and expanding markets. The idea has diffused globally – though not without resistance – that market incentives are more likely than administrative commands to encourage economic production, distribution, and exchange. In Southern Africa, as elsewhere in the world, official development strategies have been influenced by this presumption. Since the early 1980s, governments in this region have embarked, more or less voluntarily but sometimes with heavy-handed influence from international financial institutions, on programs to liberalize their economies.[2]

Yet very little is known about the attitudes of ordinary people toward economic reform. Without much empirical evidence, commentators often assert that Africans are either "for" or "against" (usually "against") liberalization.[3] But have Southern Africans even heard about their government's economic stabilization and structural adjustment programs? How do they position themselves *vis à vis* the various policies associated with such reforms? Are they satisfied with their government's performance in macro-economic management? At root, what kind of economic values do they profess: Do they believe in individual initiative or are they prone to turn to the state as the provider of public welfare? In sum, do Africans remain attached to state planning or do they embrace the risks and opportunities associated with a market economy?

We find that, in Southern Africa, people express ambivalent views about economic reform, preferring instead to steer a middle course between state and market. On one hand, they assert personal self-reliance and tolerance of risk but, on the other, they insist that the government retain a major role in economic life. They are

1. The chapter is reprinted from *World Development*, Vol 31, No 2, 2003, Michael Bratton and Robert Mattes, 'Support for Economic Reform? Popular Attitudes in Southern Africa', pp. 303–323, © (2003), with kind permission of Elsevier. The authors thank Jeremy Seekings, Nicolas van de Walle, and an anonymous reviewer for useful comments, but absolve them from any responsibility.
2. The opening volley in the market reform debate was World Bank (1981), whose progress was tracked by World Bank (1994). For contending analyses of adjustment's effects, especially on poverty, see Sahn et al. (1997) and Mkandawire and Soludo. (1999).
3. For example, Mkandawire and Olukoshi refer to the "sheer unpopularity of the programme" (1995: 3). See also Tati and Domingo, pp. 367 and 422. To be fair, the editors of this volume do distinguish between pro- and anti-reform constituencies at different locations (e.g. rural and urban) within society.

dissatisfied with the past and present performance of the economy, but optimistic about its future. And they support some policies in the structural adjustment package, but not others. On balance, popular support for market reforms is lukewarm. And it is offset, even in the context of economic growth, by a deep concern with emerging economic inequalities.

Beyond describing the extent of popular support for market reform or state-centred development in Southern Africa,[1] this chapter searches for the sources of economic attitudes. We expect that wealthier and employed people will tend to support market relations and that poverty will induce reliance on the state. Beyond a person's objective position in the socio-economic structure, however, orientations to reform will be shaped by subjective preferences. For example, we expect individuals with entrepreneurial values, plus those who positively evaluate their government's performance in economic management, to be inclined to favour open markets.

Most importantly, we situate our explanation of mass economic attitudes squarely within the historical context of Southern Africa. The region underwent a distinctive settler form of colonialism in which immigrant populations of Europeans gained control of the state from the imperial metropole. In the name of market capitalism, white settlers used state power to allocate land and jobs to themselves and to apply industrial technologies to mineral and agricultural production. Trading was often devolved to other immigrant groups, such as Indians. Majority populations of indigenous Africans were transformed into a migrant workforce and were induced to move back and forth between the white industrial heartlands and rural labour reserves, located either within domestic "homelands" or in surrounding countries.

Thus, different racial groups experienced distinctive forms of incorporation into capitalist market relations, experiences that were always mediated by the state. In addition, the countries of Southern Africa came to occupy diverse positions in an emerging regional economy, ranging from industrial hubs (for example, within South Africa, Namibia and Zimbabwe) to agrarian satellites (as in Lesotho or Malawi). These legacies of race and nation are likely to give rise to distinctive contemporary attitudes to economic reform. We predict that support for neo-liberal economic policies will be most prevalent among whites in South Africa, Namibia and Zimbabwe, and that resistance to reform will be found mainly among blacks in Botswana, Malawi and Lesotho. This is not to argue that there is something essential to race or nationality. Instead, such constructs embody, for various groups, divergent backgrounds of economic socialization through differential relations to state and market. Moreover, variations in attitudes to reform will also reflect recent political transitions in which Africans have wrested control of the state from settlers.

We favour an ecumenical explanation of economic attitudes, which casts light on the utility of various theories. Each of the following contributes a measure of expla-

1. Defined here as Botswana, Lesotho, Malawi, Namibia, South Africa, Zambia and Zimbabwe.

nation: a neo-Marxist approach that traces economic orientations to the structure of society;[1] a cultural approach that locates attitudes to reform in basic economic values;[2] and, to a lesser extent, a rationalist approach by which citizens calculate their support for reform based on the economic performance of the government of the day.[3] While all of these theories are helpful to a degree, greatest analytic leverage is achieved by a theory that emphasizes historical legacies. As Douglass North argues, "history matters...because the present and the future are connected to the past by the continuity of today's institutions. Today's and tomorrow's choices are shaped by the past."[4] In Southern Africa, the institutions of settler colonialism – and the struggles to overthrow these regimes – have shaped the economic worldviews of the region's peoples.

Data for this study are drawn from Afrobarometer surveys conducted by the authors. (For details on this, see Appendix.) These surveys asked several batteries of identical questions across seven Southern African countries between September 1999 (Zimbabwe) and July 2000 (South Africa).[5] To capture existential realities, we begin by briefly sketching living conditions. Proceeding cumulatively, we then build a series of statistical models to account for a range of popular economic attitudes. We use living conditions to predict economic evaluations; we then use living conditions and economic evaluations together to estimate economic values; and, finally, we employ all the above factors, plus historical legacies of race and nation, to build a comprehensive model of support for economic reform in Southern Africa.

The chapter concludes with implications for policy. As vividly illustrated by disputes over land ownership in Zimbabwe, attitudes to economic policy in Southern Africa have become racially charged. Whites now tend to prefer a market model of development and blacks would rather rely on the state to solve their economic grievances. Especially where recent political changes have led to majority rule (e.g. in South Africa) – though less so where economic crisis has been prolonged (e.g. in Zambia) – public opinion will push policy makers to maintain a larger role for the

---

1. A radical, progressive tradition locates the sources of opposition to market reform among the poor, the unemployed, and marginalized groups like women. For examples, see Walton and Seddon (1994), Bekker (1994), and Sarrasin (1999).

2. Cultural analysts posit that an ethic of individual achievement is a prerequisite for capitalist development and that traditional communal values constitute an obstacle to economic accumulation. Beyond the classics of Max Weber, see Shiller et.al. (1991) and Harrison and Huntington (2000).

3. Rationalists argue that economic actors form policy preferences based on self-interest; they pragmatically choose the strategies that maximize their welfare. A key theme in this literature is that support for policy or political change is predicated on tangible economic performance. For examples, see Elster (1993), Przeworski (1996), and Whitefield and Evans (1999).

4. See North (1990:vii).

5. In opting to use identical questions, a practice derived from the New Europe Barometer and Latinobarometro, we calculated gains in comparability would outweigh concerns about cultural diversity across neighbouring countries.

state in economic development than neo-classical theories of the market conventionally allow.

Living Conditions

To set the scene, we detail Southern Africans' living conditions. Specifically, we report on employment, the quality of housing, and the coverage of basic needs. These facts supplement official statistics[1] and reveal singular national features. They paint a portrait of a region in which not only AIDS, but also poverty and inequality, are common.

(a) Employment

Regarding employment, the Afrobarometer asked a three-part question. Were respondents working? If so, part-time or full-time? And if not, were they looking for work? As indicated in Table 1, unemployment is widespread in the region, ranging in a band from 33% in Zimbabwe to 45% in Botswana, but hitting 76% in Lesotho.[2] We are confident in these figures because our estimate for South Africa (36% of the workforce aged 18 years of age and above) is virtually identical to the estimate of the most recent official labour force survey.[3]

Table 1. Employment, Southern Africa, 1999–2000

	Botswana	Lesotho	Malawi	Namibia	Zambia	Zimbabwe	South Africa
Unemployed (not looking)	29	30	65	36	43	42	26
Unemployed (looking)	32	53	15	30	21	19	27
Employed, part-time (not looking)	2	1	2	2	2	6	4
Employed, part-time (looking)	7	4	2	5	5	7	10
Employed, full-time (not looking)	18	7	12	19	17	18	22
Employed, full-time (looking)	11	4	4	7	10	7	10
Don't know, refused etc.	1	1	0	1	2	1	1
Unemployment Rate	45%	76%	42%	47%	38%	33%	36%

Across the region, unemployment is significantly higher among women (52%) than men (39%). There are also big differences between rural unemployment (53%) and joblessness in the urban workforce (35%). In South Africa, many fewer blacks (41%), Coloureds (35%), and Indians (30%) have jobs than whites (8%). And the

---

1. See World Bank (2001).
2. Our unemployment estimate is derived by the following formula:
$$\frac{\% \text{ Not Working but Looking for Work}}{100\% - \% \text{ Not Working and Not Looking for Work}}$$
3. See Statistics SA (2000).

gender gap in employment (46% for women versus 29% for men) is much wider in South Africa than in the region as a whole.

Where job opportunities exist, they are often partial and temporary, especially in the region's industrial economies. Approximately one third of all current employment is part-time in Zimbabwe, Lesotho, and South Africa. Needless to say, part-time jobs do not provide full salaries and usually lack benefits. Moreover, many jobs are temporary. Across the region, 14% of those who currently enjoy full time employment say they went without a cash job for at least one month in the previous year, a figure that rises to 18% in Zambia and 22% in Lesotho. Four in ten Southern Africans (40%) with part time jobs were unemployed during the previous year.

(b) Housing and household services

Afrobarometer fieldworkers also observed the quality of people's shelter. The proportion of the population living in unimproved "traditional" housing, commonly constructed of mud and thatch, varies greatly across the region (see Table 2). More than one-third of the population occupies traditional houses in Namibia, Malawi, and Zambia, compared with less than one in ten in Botswana and South Africa. Improved houses – for example, with cement or brick walls, windows (sometimes with glazing), and metal or tile roofs – are most common in Botswana and available to more than half the population in all countries except Namibia.

Table 2. Shortages of Basic Needs, Southern Africa, 1999–2000

	Botswana	Lesotho	Malawi	Namibia	Zambia	Zimbabwe	S. Africa
Shelter	6	4	5	14	13	16	5
Enough fuel to heat your home or cook your food	31	43	29	41	38	40	28
Enough clean water with which to drink and cook	16	46	30	47	50	41	24
Medicine or medical treatment that you needed.	16	38	49	58	69	54	38
Enough food to eat	49	60	38	54	61	50	34
A cash income	52	77	69	69	80	71	47

Sub-standard shelter in the form of temporary shack-type dwellings is most common in countries with an *apartheid* legacy of population displacement like Namibia and South Africa. Unsurprisingly, race and shelter are closely associated, not only in South Africa, but across the region.[1] Over 95% of whites live in improved houses,

---

1. Beside 320 interviews with white respondents in South Africa, an additional 125 were scattered across Namibia, Botswana, Zambia and Zimbabwe. 220 interviews with people of mixed race ("Coloureds") were conducted in South Africa, and another 60 mostly in Namibia, but a handful each in Malawi, Zimbabwe and Zambia. Finally 100 interviews with Asians were conducted in South Africa, plus another 8 in Namibia, Botswana and Zimbabwe.

as do Asians. By contrast, only 62% of blacks live in improved houses and virtually all those living in traditional houses or temporary structures are black.

Slightly different patterns apply for household services. South Africans enjoy the best access in the region to piped water and electricity, though substantial proportions in Botswana and Zimbabwe also obtain these services. Only in South Africa and Botswana do large majorities of people have water delivered to their household or compound (68 and 58% respectively). Beside these two countries, the figures run from 39% in Zimbabwe to just 7% in Lesotho. The South African result represents a massive increase in the availability of piped household water over the last few years since, as recently as 1995, the government estimated that only 21% had piped water in the household.[1]

Moreover, only in South Africa do substantial proportions of households enjoy access to electricity. The survey figure (78%) actually outstrips the original target set by South Africa's Reconstruction and Development Program (RDP) in 1994 (72% by 2000).[2] Elsewhere in the region, the figures run from 42% (Zimbabwe) to just 4% in Lesotho. Overall, people living in Lesotho have fewer household services than anyone else in the region, including even Namibians, Zambians, and Malawians.

(c) Poverty

In order to measure poverty, we presented survey respondents with a list of basic needs and asked: "In the last twelve months, how often have you or your family gone without (these things)?"[3] Table 2 displays the proportions of people who say that they "sometimes" or "often" do without.

Southern Africans were most likely to have been short of cash income (on average, 66%) and least likely to experience homelessness (9%).[4] Between these extremes, significant proportions of people sometimes or often went without food (an average of 49%), medical treatment (46%), clean water (36%), and fuel for heating or cooking (36%).

Cross-national differences in the nature of poverty are partly related to each country's natural resource endowment.[5] For example, Basotho (citizens of Lesotho) are most likely to report shortages of fuel for heating homes and cooking food,

---

1. Republic of South Africa (1995) and Stavrou (2000: 143).

2. Stavrou (2000: 152).

3. This approach to living conditions – measuring what people have to do without, rather than what they have – is broadly based on Rose (1998) and Rose and Haerpfer (1998).

4. These estimates almost assuredly underestimate the true rate of homelessness since they are derived from a *household* based sample. In other words, Afrobarometer interviewers only selected people currently living in households.

5. At the bivariate levels, cross-national differences account for just over 10% of the variance in personal experience with poverty (Eta Squared = .12; Eta =.35, sig. = .001).

reflecting the sparse supplies of natural firewood in this high-altitude country. And Namibians, who contend with the most arid environment in the region, are very likely to lack access to a reliable household water supply. However, Zambians consistently report the most frequent shortfalls of water, health care, food and income, implying that this country suffers the most extensive, integrated, and deep-seated poverty. In Zambia's case, however, widespread poverty appears to derive less from the natural environment – which is relatively bountiful – than from the under-performance of its development bureaucracy. The fact that well managed development programs can overcome an unpromising natural resource base is illustrated by Botswana's strong record of meeting felt needs for clean water and health care.

The demographic distribution of poverty within South Africa is revealing. Along every dimension of basic need, reported shortages follow the racial rankings imposed by *apartheid*. Black respondents say they are more needy than Coloured and Indian respondents, who in turn report more unfulfilled needs than whites. These racial differences also suggest that people's responses to these questions reflect absolute need rather than relative deprivation. It might be expected that wealthier people would adjust and expand their definition of what constitutes "enough" food, or water, or medical treatment. However, if this were so, more white South Africans would complain that they were not able to obtain these items, which is not the case.

For summary purposes, we constructed an *index of poverty* based on the respondent's access to the basic goods and services listed in Table 2. The index enables us to infer an average poverty score for each person, or for each country.[1] Besides having statistical convenience, this scale demonstrates that respondents who report regular shortages on one item are likely to report shortages on all the rest. In short, poverty is a mutually reinforcing web of deprivations.

We then sought to explain the prevalence of poverty across the region using multivariate regression analysis. In this case, a small set of variables measuring employment, rural-urban location, level of formal education, age, gender, race, and nationality accounts for just over one-quarter of the variance in the overall poverty measure (see Appendix, Model A). When all such factors are controlled simultaneously, education has the largest impact on poverty of any measured variable. Other things being equal, the more people have been exposed to formal education, the less likely they are to lack basic needs. At the same time, urban dwellers are much less likely to experience poverty than rural Southern Africans. Employment is also strongly associated with lower levels of poverty. Beyond obvious implications, this

---

1. This scale was verified through factor and reliability analyses, which indicated that the item on homelessness should be removed, but that the rest of the items formed one factor that explained 49% of the total variance (Eigenvalue = 2.46) and a reliability score (Kronbach's Alpha) of .74. The item that most strongly defined the scale was cash shortages (a loading of .71) and the weakest was water shortages (with a loading of .50).

finding draws attention to the absence of official programs of unemployment benefits across the region (except in South Africa), and the very limited impact of these benefits in keeping the unemployed out of poverty.

Moreover, significant cross-national and racial differences remain. Controlling for education or employment does not eliminate the impact of race or citizenship.[1] Compared to black respondents across the region, being white, Coloured or Indian is associated with sharply reduced levels of poverty, largely reflecting the impact of *apartheid* privileges in South Africa, Namibia, and Zimbabwe. And, compared to South Africans, being a resident of Botswana is associated with a *reduction* in poverty. However, being from Zambia, Zimbabwe, Namibia, and Lesotho is associated with an *increase* in poverty.

Economic Evaluations

How do Southern Africans view current economic conditions in their countries? The Afrobarometer surveys asked respondents to evaluate current national economic conditions, recent trends and future prospects, and their personal economic situations compared to other citizens.

(a) Economic satisfaction

Across Southern Africa, the end of the millenium (1999–2000) was seen as a tough time. In no country was a majority of citizens satisfied with the current condition of the national economy (see Table 3). Only in Namibia did more respondents proclaim themselves satisfied than dissatisfied, though large proportions felt uninformed or were undecided. Everywhere else the economic mood was negative, overwhelmingly so in Zimbabwe, but also markedly too in Lesotho and Zambia. Even in Botswana, which possesses the highest per capita gross national product in the region after South Africa, less than one-third of respondents were content with national economic conditions.

These negative assessments appear to be based on comparisons with the past. In other words, people are dissatisfied with national economic conditions in part because they think, "things ain't what they used to be". Evidence for this interpretation can be found in the extremely high correlation between contemporary and retrospective economic assessments.[2] In other words, those who are dissatisfied with current economic conditions also think that economic conditions have recently worsened. Again, Namibians were the only Southern Africans to consider that their

---

1. An individual's level of poverty was regressed on gender, age, employment, education and rural/urban status, as well as a series of dummy variables measuring race (with black as the excluded group for comparison) and country (with South Africa as the excluded group).
2. Pearson's correlation = .750, sig. =.000.

economy was on an upward trajectory. In this instance, Batswana (citizens of Botswana), who experienced the highest quality of life and GNP growth rates in the sample during the 1990s, tended to see their economy as essentially holding steady. All other Southern Africans perceived economic declines over the previous year.

Table 3. Satisfaction with Current National Economic Conditions, Southern Africa, 1999–2000

	Botswana	Lesotho	Malawi	Namibia	Zambia	Zimbabwe	S. Africa
Very dissatisfied / dissatisfied	55	77	69	30	74	94	68
Neither dissatisfied nor satisfied	9	4	4	16	6	3	16
Satisfied / very satisfied	32	12	26	41	19	3	15
Don't know	4	8	1	14	2	1	2

What about the future? Cross-national patterns begin to change slightly when people are asked about their prospective economic expectations. While Namibians remained the most optimistic (44%), a slight plurality of Batswana also believed that their economy would improve over the next 12 months (31%). Zimbabweans again anchored the bottom of the scale: in late 1999 they could hardly have been more pessimistic: only 6% expected the national economy to get better anytime soon.

As Table 4 shows, a turnabout in popular expectations has occurred in South Africa. Except after a monetary crisis in mid-1998, public optimism about the country's economic future has always been quite high, particularly among black South Africans. The August 2000 Afrobarometer results, however, represent a significant decline in economic confidence. While optimism decreased among South Africans of all races, among blacks it plunged from 63% in April 1999 to 34% in mid-2000.

Table 4. Evaluations of the National Economy in South Africa, 1995 to 2000

	Sept / Nov 1995	June / July 1997	September 1998	Oct / Nov 1998	Feb / March 1999	April 1999	Aug / Sept 2000
Past Year	30	27	25	32	29	31	15
Present	NA	21	17	25	20	20	15
Future	NA	44	34	50	47	51	29

(b) Relative deprivation

Turning from national economic conditions, we asked whether each individual's economic conditions are seen as "worse, the same as, or better" than the conditions of other people in their country. Often called relative deprivation, this interpersonal comparison has been identified by public opinion researchers as a key determinant of political behaviour.[1]

---

1. See for example, Gurr (1970).

In every country except Namibia, most respondents saw themselves as worse off than their fellow citizens. The constituency expressing relative deprivation was an absolute majority in five countries: Botswana, Lesotho, Malawi, Zimbabwe, and Zambia. The inclusion of Botswana on this list suggests that, at least from a subjective perspective, economic growth in that country has not eliminated perceptions of social inequality. Economic growth, applied unevenly, may have raised expectations and highlighted disparities. In other words, it is quite possible for citizens to feel relatively worse off even as their country does better.

Two important points emerge for South Africa, which ranks as one of the most unequal societies in the world, second only to Brazil. Yet one-third of the South African respondents say that they are doing "about as same as others", the highest proportion in the region. This suggests that, when making comparisons with others, South Africans refer primarily to people in their own communities (which, because of *apartheid* housing patterns, means people from their own race group) rather than comparing themselves with historically advantaged whites. In fact, since 1997, the levels of relative deprivation expressed by black South Africans have actually been *lower* than other groups, an apparently astounding inversion of economic realities in that country.

At the same time, however, the proportion of South Africans, especially blacks, who feel relatively deprived has increased sharply since 1997. One possible explanation is that the government's structural adjustment package and the accelerated development of a black middle class have exacerbated intra-racial inequalities. In absolute terms, there are now more blacks than whites in the top two categories in the country's official Living Standards Measure. And by most estimates, the gap between poor and wealthy blacks is now wider than between whites and blacks as a whole. The increased visibility of income inequalities among blacks may well have begun to generate a growing sense of deprivation and frustration amongst those left behind.

(c) Management of the economy

What do Southern Africans think about government performance in managing the economy? Economic dissatisfaction is matched, at best, by lukewarm evaluations (see Table 5). In only two countries (Botswana and Namibia) does government receive, on balance, a positive rating in most policy areas. Given their political and economic crisis, Zimbabweans are extremely negative.

Table 5. Public Evaluations of Government's Economic Performance, Southern Africa, 1999–2000

	Botswana	Zimbabwe	Zambia	Malawi	Lesotho	Namibia	South Africa
Creating jobs	52	20	26	32	38	47	10
Ensuring that prices remain stable	41	14	28	8	20	38	17
Improving health services	69	35	37	46	50	62	43
Addressing the educational needs of all	71	46	43	62	57	62	49
Managing the economy	60	16	33	25	36	45	28
Delivering basic services (water, electricity)	69	36	40	65	35	55	61
Average	60	28	35	40	39	52	35

Across the region, governments are rated most favourably for delivering education (a cross-national average of 55% approval), water and electricity (52%) and health services (52%). Government performance in controlling inflation (24%) receives the lowest average score across countries, and in each country is one of the three most unpopular performance areas. And only one third of Southern Africans think their governments are performing well at job creation and macro-economic management.

(d) Explaining economic evaluations

Why were Southern Africans so melancholy about economic trends in 1999–2000? Was it due to subjective assessments of their personal or national economic situations?

We first constructed an *index of national economic evaluations* that summarizes present, retrospective, and prospective evaluations.[1] We then used multiple regression analysis to examine the collective and individual impact of a range of factors including the living conditions described earlier (employment, quality of housing, and poverty), standard demographic indicators (country of residence, race, rural-urban status, and gender), and individual awareness (extent of formal education, level of interest in politics, and the extent to which people use newspapers and television for news).

The results are somewhat surprising. To be sure, the greater a person's level of poverty, the less he or she is satisfied with national economic conditions and trends (see Appendix, Model B). But it makes no difference to economic satisfaction as to whether one is employed, lives in a good house, is rural or urban, educated or uneducated. Nor does it matter how much one uses the news media, though there is a very slight impact from being interested in politics and public affairs. Instead, we see the persistent impact of cross-national and racial differences, now on the index of national economic evaluations. All other things being equal, white and Asian respondents are significantly more pessimistic than blacks. Namibians are consider-

---

1. Factor analysis extracted one factor underlying retrospective, present and prospective economic evaluations. The factor explains 73% of the common variance (Eigenvalue = 2.19). The three items load almost equally on the factor (all above .70).

ably more optimistic than South Africans, while Zimbabweans are considerably less optimistic.

What leads a person to feel relatively deprived? In search of an answer, we regressed perceptions of relative deprivation on the same set of independent variables (see Appendix, Model C). Unsurprisingly, the most important factor is poverty: the more one suffers shortages of basic necessities, the more deprived one feels compared to other citizens. More interestingly, greater exposure to news media, higher levels of formal education, and higher levels of interest in politics are also all associated with *lower* levels of relative deprivation. At first glance, this may seem counterintuitive since greater awareness of how the rest of the country is doing might be expected to increase relative deprivation. But it appears that heightened exposure to the national media as well as more education enables people to understand challenges facing the whole country and to conclude that all are in the same boat.

Again, important racial and national differences remain even after other factors are taken into account. Extraordinarily, white and Indian respondents are more likely to perceive relative deprivation than blacks, indicating once more that people tend to refer to their own, rather than other, groups when making such comparisons. Zimbabweans and Basotho are more likely to feel relatively deprived than South Africans. And Namibians, Malawians and Zambians are less likely to feel this way.

Finally, what factors are associated with popular evaluations of government economic performance? To answer this, we first constructed a summary *index of government economic performance* that provides a reliable average score of popular evaluations across the six areas of economic policy (see Table 5).[1] Regressing these scores on the same set of independent variables, we find that the poor are less likely to approve of government economic performance (see Appendix, Model D). Interestingly, those with full-time jobs are also less likely to approve of government performance, as are urban respondents and older respondents. In terms of awareness, higher levels of formal education lead to lower levels of approval, but higher levels of media use lead to greater approval. Taking all other factors into account, white, Coloured and Indian respondents are less approving of government economic management than blacks. *Ceteris paribus,* Namibians and Batswana are more satisfied with their governments' performance than are South Africans, while Zimbabweans are less satisfied than South Africans.

These findings are both encouraging and sobering. In a region marked by widespread poverty, it is encouraging that popular assessments of economic conditions

---

1. Factor analysis indicated that these six items form one valid factor that explains 55% of the total variance (Eigenvalue = 3.72) with a reliability score (Kronbach's Alpha) of .83. The item that most strongly defined the scale was government performance providing health care (a loading of .76) and the weakest was the provision of water and electricity (.57).

or government economic management are not simply reflections of personal circumstances, though they are certainly shaped by them. People draw distinctions between how they personally are doing and the overall direction and management of the national economy. People without jobs or good housing do not feel substantially worse about economic conditions and prospects than their more privileged counterparts, suggesting that they have not abandoned hope. This disconnection between personal circumstances, national trends, and approval of government performance provides political elites with a measure of leeway, since it moderates political demands.

But the other side of this coin is that citizens may be hard to satisfy. Even when people do find jobs, are able to afford better housing, or escape poverty, they do not become any more optimistic about the economy or government performance. To arrive at economic evaluations, they apparently look to a larger set of factors than the health of their household budget.[1] For example, even if economies are growing, Southern Africans remain concerned that the benefits of growth are not being distributed evenly.

Persistent racial differences in economic satisfaction are probably related to the effects of the drastic turnabout in political and economic power that have occurred in South Africa and Namibia and, to a lesser extent, Zimbabwe. Even at the same levels of education or economic status, people of different races see themselves and the country going in very different directions. Blacks and whites compare present trends and government performance not just with the previous year, but with how life used to be under a previous segregated regime. Across a whole range of areas, the same government policies (employment equity, to name just one example) have very different implications for the interests of white and black workers. In addition, racial stereotypes of black government may colour minority groups' level of confidence in a majority-dominated government's ability to run the economy.

Finally, enduring cross-national differences reflect macro-level trends in particular countries that are not captured by indicators of personal economic circumstances. For instance, the consistently negative impact of living in Zimbabwe is a good example. Regardless of real changes in personal circumstances, the policies of the Mugabe government have drastically undermined Zimbabwean views of the country's economic prospects and stretched popular patience to the limits.

Economic Values

Where do Southern Africans position themselves in the great debate over the roles of state and market in economic development? Do people see themselves as autonomous economic agents, or do they prefer to rely on government for well-being?

---

1. For more on the role of "sociotropic" economic evaluations, see Kinder and Kiewet (1981).

Does enduring poverty lead Southern Africans to value state activism and regulation, or alternatively, have failed efforts at state planning created a receptive audience for neo-liberal economic policies, even among the poor? Given the history of settler colonialism in this region, one would expect that Africans (as opposed to racial minorities) would be especially attached to the state as an instrument for correcting *apartheid*-type inequities.

(a) Self-reliance or dependence?

To explore economic values, Afrobarometer surveys first asked respondents to choose between two options: should ordinary people be responsible for their own success in life, or should government take the main responsibility for ensuring public welfare? The results are mixed (see Table 6). At one extreme stands Malawi, where almost three-quarters value self-reliance; at the other end is Zimbabwe, where just over one-third does so. If there is any regional tendency, it is for a slight majority to favour self-reliance (a cross national average of 51%), as illustrated by the pattern of public preferences in Botswana, Zambia, and South Africa. But, across most of Southern Africa, we find significant minorities who would prefer the state to act as the guarantor of improved living conditions.

Table 6. Self-Reliance versus Dependence, Southern Africa, 1999–2000

	Botswana	Lesotho	Malawi	Namibia	Zambia	Zimbabwe	S. Africa
People should be responsible for their own success and well being.	48	43	73	54	50	37	52
Do not agree with either	4	2	2	1	1	3	1
Government should bear the main responsibility for ensuring the success and well being of people.	43	53	25	40	43	59	47
Don't know	6	2	0	5	5	1	1

Totals may not equal 100 per cent due to rounding.

What explains any cross-national differences? The frequency of self-reliant sentiments is essentially unrelated to a country's level of national wealth, the growth rate of its economy, or the proportions of its population employed in agriculture or industry. Instead, based on the contrasting cases of Malawi and Zimbabwe, self-reliance appears to be connected to the prevailing policy regime. Historically, the government of Malawi – especially under the minimalist economic policies of Hastings Banda – provided relatively few services to its predominantly rural population of self-provisioning peasants. In Zimbabwe after 1980, however, the Mugabe government embarked on major spending programmes to extend agricultural, educational and medical programmes to the rural hinterlands, the political base of the ZANU-PF party. These distinctive policy regimes, and the politicians' promises that accompanied them, have helped to create divergent expectations about the extent to which people can rely on government.

(b) Opportunity or equality?

If people use their own initiative to get ahead economically, one likely result is that some will gain more than others. Given the egalitarian nature of African traditions, it might be expected that there would be little popular tolerance for income inequalities. To tap this, we again asked respondents to choose between two options: Should people be free to earn as much as they can, even if this leads to large differences of income? Or should government place limits on how much rich people can earn, even if this discourages some people from working hard?

Southern Africans were surer in this instance. In six out of seven countries (and by absolute majorities in five of the six), more people valued freedom to maximize income than wanted income limits. This suggests a need to reconsider, or at least temper, claims about egalitarian preferences among Africans.[1] Once more, Malawians were the most economically liberal and Zimbabweans expressed the most communitarian views. Given widespread unemployment in the region and its strong connection to poverty, we wondered whom respondents held responsible for creating jobs: the government or themselves. The same general patterns obtained with Malawians and Namibians exhibiting strong preferences for individual entrepreneurship; however, majorities preferred government job provision in South Africa, Lesotho and, again, Zimbabwe.

(c) Tolerance for economic risk

In a market economy, reward often entails risk. We were curious whether Southern Africans would stake personal resources in the quest for private incomes, say by investing their household savings or loans in a business. Or would they avoid starting a new enterprise because it might lose money?

In this case, respondents cast doubt aside. Everywhere, clear majorities (over 75% in five countries) said that they would risk money by investing in a personal enterprise. While Malawi again led the pack, even Zimbabweans strongly favoured the entrepreneurial option. Indeed the findings are so overwhelmingly risk-oriented that we are led to query whether they are accurate, especially since vulnerability is supposed to make poor people averse to risk.[2] On one hand, the choice to invest capital may be too hypothetical for many respondents to envisage. Or they may take

---

1. In Julius Nyerere's words, "We in Africa have no more need of being taught socialism than we have of being taught democracy. Both are rooted in our past, in the traditional society which produced us." (1968), p.12.

2. For a recent contribution, see Dercon (2000). At the same time, while we do find a relationship, the bivariate association is very modest if not weak between risk acceptance (reduced to a two point scale) and poverty (Pearson's $r = -.11$, sig $= .01$).

a relaxed attitude to borrowing, thinking that it only jeopardizes someone else's money. On the other hand, tolerance for economic risk may be more widespread than usually thought, with Southern Africans being eager for opportunities to start businesses.

(d) State or market?

Are these expressions of economic individualism matched by preferences for markets (rather than states) as the appropriate principle for organizing the macro-economy? Not necessarily. The Afrobarometer reveals various ways in which people remain committed to a substantial economic role for the state and express scepticism about free markets.

Respondents were asked to say who should take the main responsibility for delivering a list of important economic services: Should it be government, private business, individuals, or some combination of these providers? Table 7 shows that people overwhelmingly prefer the state to take charge. First, a majority in every Southern African country wants government to be responsible for providing seasonal agricultural credit to farmers (at a regional average of 67%). This preference reflects a well-founded conviction that private banks will rarely make loans to medium- and small-scale agricultural producers. Second, almost as many people (63%) want government to be the principal dispenser of schools and health clinics. Knowing that faith-based service providers (e.g. mission stations) have greatly reduced coverage of these services in recent years, people may have a hard time even imagining affordable private sector alternatives to government schools and clinics. As such, the majority of citizens are consistently committed to public education and medicine as the preferred modalities in every country.

Table 7. Preference for Public Provision of Services, Southern Africa 1999–2000

	Botswana	Lesotho	Malawi	Namibia	Zambia	Zimbabwe	S. Africa
Helping farmers borrow money	76	84	70	51	76	62	53
Providing schools and clinics	67	69	50	72	57	53	76
Buying and selling [the main national commodity]	77	49	38	43	75	42	45
Creating jobs	48	74	52	41	57	48	47
Building houses	35	45	28	40	44	35	63

Third, though by a slimmer majority (53%), Southern Africans even prefer that the government direct the marketing of the country's main export commodity.[1] This is a somewhat surprising result given the poor performance of many parastatal marketing boards in operating profitably in sagging international crop and mineral markets

---

1. The actual commodity mentioned in the question differed from country to country: Botswana and Namibia – diamonds; Lesotho – water; Malawi and Zimbabwe – tobacco; South Africa – gold.; Zambia – copper.

in the 1970s and 1980s. It also indicates that the privatization of public corporations, or the liberalization of their markets during the 1990s, has not met with widespread public approval. Only in Malawi does public sentiment tilt toward the involvement of private businesses or individual merchants in commodity trading, in this case in the buying and selling of burley tobacco. Perhaps people are more inclined to experiment with alternative marketing arrangements for a smallholder cash crop than with a country's strategic mineral resource.

Fourth, by a similar margin (52%), people see the government as responsible for providing employment. Only 7% regard the private sector (businesses and individuals) as the rightful providers, though 40% consider job creation as a shared public–private responsibility. Basotho, who possess few paid alternatives to migrant labor, display the heaviest commitment to public employment. Not surprisingly, people are likely to regard individual or corporate entrepreneurs as job providers in the countries that have large private sectors. Indeed, absolute majorities (over 50%) see job creation as a shared public–private responsibility in Botswana, Namibia, South Africa, and Zimbabwe.

Finally, house construction is broadly seen as a private responsibility, the only economic function on the list that is so regarded. Across the region, an average of just 41% regards domestic dwelling construction as a government duty. The regional norm is pulled up by South Africa, the one country where a majority of people (63%) think that the state is obliged to build houses. This orientation reflects both the policy legacy of *apartheid*, in which public construction projects were a cornerstone of residential segregation, and the ANC-government's crash program of house building begun in 1994 under the RDP. Otherwise, most people in the region think housing is most properly provided by individuals operating in an open market, rather than by the state. On this issue, Malawians, along with Batswana and Zimbabweans, are the most market-oriented.

(e) Explaining economic values

What shapes these economic values? Are they simply a function of an individual's living conditions, with poor people more likely to depend on government? Or are values affected by economic evaluations? For example, does dissatisfaction with a government mismanagement of the economy lead people to prefer an expanded role for markets?

To find answers, we first created an *index of personal economic independence* that summarizes respondents' values on self-reliance, job creation, and freedom to earn.[1] We regressed the index on our standard set of independent variables (see Appendix, Model E).

As expected, poor people are less likely to value personal economic independence and more likely to turn to the state for welfare.[2] Conversely, greater cognitive engagement with the political and economic worlds (as measured by formal education, exposure to news media, interest in politics, and political efficacy) increases personal economic independence. Also, those who are more satisfied with government management of the economy and with national economic trends are more likely to value independence while those who feel economically deprived are less likely to do so. Yet, once again, significant cross-national differences remain even after controlling for all the factors just mentioned. Citizens of every country except Zimbabwe are more likely to value personal economic independence than are South Africans. Also, whites are more likely to value autonomy than blacks, even after controlling for all other factors.

To explore why Southern Africans seem to prefer states above markets in the provision of most economic services we developed an *index of preference for service provision*. It summarizes preferences for private versus public delivery mechanisms for six policies (agricultural credit, schools and clinics, export marketing, job creation, reducing crime, and building houses).[3] We then used the same set of independent variables to try and predict the index (see Appendix, Model F).

Again, those who endure poverty are less likely to prefer private provision of economic services, though employment status and housing conditions make no difference. Similarly, exposure to information leads to greater preference for private provision. In fact, formal education and media use are even stronger predictors than

1. Because respondents tended to agree "strongly" rather than "somewhat" with these statements, thus concentrating responses on the extremities of four-point scales, we reduced them to two-point scales combining "strongly agree" and "agree" with each statement. Factor analysis indicated that the item on risk acceptance did not fit with these three items, but that the rest of the items formed one factor that explained 52% of the total variance (Eigenvalue = 1.55), though with a barely acceptable reliability score (Kronbach's Alpha) of .53. The item that most strongly defined the scale was self-reliance (a loading of .67) and the weakest was government regulation of earnings (with a loading of .41). Ordinarily, we would only use indices with a reliability of .60, but the effectiveness of this construct in helping to explain popular support for economic reform (as discussed below), argued for its inclusion in the analysis.

2. Recall that poverty is measured using the index of poverty (i.e. shortages of five basic needs). Note that the respondent's employment status and housing conditions make no meaningful difference.

3. In order to create this scale, we constructed new items with a score of 1 if the person favored government provision, 2 if they favored any form of public-private partnership, and 3 if they favoured solely private provision. Factor analysis indicated that all the items formed one unrotated factor that explains 35.5% of the common variance with a reliability (Kronbach's Alpha) of .63. The item that most strongly defined the scale was job creation (factor loading of .57) and the weakest was marketing of key export commodities (.37).

poverty, each leading to increased attachment to liberal policy approaches. Cross-national (and some racial) differences also play an independent role. Controlling for all other factors, citizens of every country except Botswana and Zambia are more likely than South Africans to favour the delivery of services by private agencies. This finding suggests that Botswana's economic miracle has induced a well-founded preference for public sector provision among its population. As expected, however, whites and Asians are more likely to prefer private provision than blacks, reflecting for example a transfer of their allegiance to private schools and clinics as educational and medical service have been opened up to all races.

Support for Economic Reform

Finally, we consider what Southern Africans think about policies of economic stabilization and structural adjustment. An obvious starting point is to ask whether people have ever heard about their country's economic reform program. Because there was no identifiable program in Botswana, Lesotho and Namibia, we can only present responses for four countries.

(a) Awareness of adjustment programs

There is more variation in awareness of adjustment programs than on any other item studied here.[1] At one extreme, almost all Zimbabweans (85%) claim to have heard of the country's Economic Structural Adjustment Program, known colloquially as ESAP. Introduced in 1991, ESAP aimed at liberalizing trade by reducing import tariffs and providing incentives to promote exports. But the implementation of reform failed to stave off recession or to reduce budget deficits and inflation, notably in food prices.[2] The government blamed these consequences on the World Bank and International Monetary Fund, at whose instigation the adjustment programs had been introduced. As such, ESAP terminology entered public discourse and popular culture ("Elastic Stomach Adjustment Program!", "Eat Sadza And Perish!"), including pop songs.[3] Thus, many Zimbabweans learned about the program, usually attaching to it a negative connotation.

At the other extreme, only 13% of South Africans recognize the Growth, Employment and Redistribution policy, commonly known as GEAR. This stands in stark contrast to the program's visibility in elite debate. Launched in 1996, GEAR was a home-grown policy that was consistent with the preferences of international financial institutions, foreign investors, and the local business community. It aimed at export-led growth, a fiscally disciplined public budget, a flexible labor market, and

---

1. The contingency coefficient for SAP awareness by country is .832, sig. = .000.

2. See Mlambo (1997), Dashwood (2000), and Jenkins and Knight (2002).

3. Vambe (2000: 80–81).

privatization.[1] It consistently drew ire from the governing African National Congress's allies: the South African Congress of Trade Unions and the South African Communist Party. Perhaps because GEAR downplayed social redistribution in favour of economic growth, it never gained the public currency of the RDP. Indeed, by claiming that GEAR was simply a means to implement RDP goals, the government never actively publicized the adjustment program that was the cornerstone of its macro-economic strategy. It is in this context of adjustment by stealth that South Africans' stunningly low public awareness of GEAR must be understood.

Malawi and Zambia are more representative of the region as a whole in that about half of the adult population have heard of the national economic structural adjustment program and about half have not. Policy makers should nonetheless be disappointed: after years of sustained efforts to induce governments to reorient economies toward the market, large proportions of intended beneficiaries in at least three Southern African countries claim to be ignorant that such a strategy even exists. On the other hand, politicians might see this as a blessing; public awareness of the government's adoption of an adjustment program may be damaging because, even if never implemented, it signals the government's weakness in the face of international pressure.[2]

Beyond mere name recognition, however, Southern Africans undoubtedly experience the consequences of specific policy reforms in their daily lives. In the next section we break down a typical reform package by asking people whether they support or reject various component policies.

(b) Support for economic reform

Economic reform involves a complex package of price and institutional adjustments that are rarely implemented in a single phase and which citizens do not have to accept or reject wholesale. Southern Africans regularly encounter four such policies: user fees for services, market pricing for consumer goods, privatization of public companies, and reductions in civil service employment.

First, we examine popular preferences regarding user fees. A major goal of economic stabilization is to cut public budget deficits, for instance by introducing cost-sharing in the provision of public services. Users are asked to pay a fee that helps to offset the real cost of service delivery. Throughout the region, fees have been introduced for basic health care services, which require outpatients to contribute to the cost of medical consultations or prescription drugs.

We asked respondents to choose: Is it better to be able to visit clinics and get medicines for free, even if the standards of health care are low? Or is it better to

---

1. Republic of South Africa (1996). For commentary on GEAR, see Bratton and Landsberg (2000) and Natrass and Seekings (2001).
2. O'Donnell (1999).

raise health care standards, even if you have to pay medical fees?[1] Perhaps unexpectedly, more people preferred the reform option (impose fees, raise standards) to the *status quo ante* (no fees, low standards) in all seven countries (see Table 8, line 1). In some places the reform constituency was far larger than the anti-reform faction (Lesotho, Botswana and South Africa) but in other places the reform majority was slim (Malawi and Namibia). Despite the fact that people grumble about the burden of paying user fees for social services, they are nonetheless willing to do so. In return, however, they insist that standards of services must rise.

Table 8. Support for Economic Reform, Southern Africa, 1999–2000

	Botswana	Lesotho	Malawi	Namibia	Zambia	Zimbabwe	S. Africa
Support User Fees	56	66	48	49	51	58	59
Support Market Pricing	50	38	41	45	59	43	49
Support Privatization	49	29	32	31	29	42	44
Support Civil Service Retrenchment	21	23	21	20	34	51	43
MEAN: Support Adjustment (Rank)	44 (3)	39 (5)	36 (6)	36 (6)	43 (4)	49 (1)	49 (1)

Percentage agreeing "somewhat" or "strongly", derived from previous tables.

Second, we looked at attitudes to market pricing. In several countries in the 1980s, subsidies for staple foodstuffs and other basic consumer goods ballooned to the largest item in the government budget. Economic stabilization has required the removal of such subsidies, allowing prices to find their own levels in the marketplace. One happy side effect of "getting the prices right" for consumer goods is that supplies usually expand to meet demand, thus putting an end to policy-induced shortages. Goods flood onto once-empty supermarket shelves. While consumers assuredly face higher prices for these items, they no longer have to queue up in the early hours of the morning, as Zambians did to buy bread.

The survey choice here was: Is it better to have a variety of goods available in the market, even if prices are high? Or is it better to have low prices, even if there are shortages of goods? In this instance we find a measure of support for market-oriented reform, but it is far from resounding. To be sure, people prefer market pricing to commodity shortages in four countries (Botswana, Namibia, Zambia, and South Africa) (see Table 8, line 2). Evidence of popular support for "getting the prices right" is offset by the fact that this policy reform is supported by a clear majority in only one country: Zambia. The exception of Zambia is probably due to popular memories of severe policy-induced shortages during the 1980s, leading Zambians to reject the hardships associated with the old economic regime. Moreover, as liberalization reforms have permitted Zambians to enter trading *en masse*, they have come

---

1. On the wording of the user fee question, and all other questions about reform policies, respondents were not forced to choose between unrealistic options. If they wished, they could opt for "agree with neither" or "don't know". On average, however, fewer than one in ten did so.

to support market pricing as sellers rather than simply as buyers. In Zimbabwe, Lesotho and Malawi, however, where markets were never so distorted as to lead to supply bottlenecks for staple foods (at least until 2002 in Zimbabwe), people remain more solidly attached to price controls.

Third, we turn to public opinion on privatization. Should the government sell its factories, businesses and farms to private companies and individuals? Or should it retain ownership of these enterprises? The Southern African responses on this item amount to a strong anti-reform reaction. In contrast to support for policy efforts to stabilize public budgets, we find little popular backing for the institutional transformations associated with economic structural adjustment. For example, there is scant mass enthusiasm for the state to divest itself of public corporations. Nowhere in the region do majorities favour privatization (Table 8, line 3). In many places, this policy is rejected by a large margin. In Zambia, for example, where the survey took place shortly before the government finalized its sale of the copper mines, two out of three citizens opposed the divestment of public companies. Only in Botswana (where the diamond mines have long been under joint ownership) do more people prefer privatization.[1]

Fourth, and finally, we examine attitudes to public sector reform. Many economists now acknowledge that political and managerial innovations are necessary in order to restore growth to African economies. Even international financial institutions have come to include good governance initiatives in their adjustment and poverty alleviation programs.[2] A core element is the rehabilitation of run-down civil service institutions by reducing the size of the personnel establishment and improving professionalism and efficiency. Inevitably, some public employees lose their jobs in the process, even as others become better trained, better paid, and better motivated.

To get at this aspect of public sector reform, respondents were asked to opt for one of the following statements. Either "The government cannot afford so many public employees, so it should lay some of them off"; or "All civil servants should keep their jobs, even if paying their salaries is costly to the country." The results (Table 8, line 4) show that there is even less support for civil service retrenchment (on average, 32%) than for privatization (37%), with barely one out of five people in four countries supporting this policy. The only exception is Zimbabwe, where more than half approve of retrenchment. Our interpretation of this anomaly is that Zimbabweans are reacting against the abusive patronage practices of ZANU-PF which

---

1. Citing low world prices, a factor that does not affect Botswana diamonds sold through the de Beers cartel, Anglo-American corporation withdrew from its copper-mining interests in Zambia after just two years of privatised ownership. At the time of writing, the Zambian government was trying to keep the mines open while it searched for another buyer. See *New York Times*, August 19, 2002.
2. For example, World Bank (2000).

have bloated government bodies with unqualified political appointees and closed public employment to those deemed politically disloyal.

In sum, we find that Southern Africans support some market-oriented policy reforms, but oppose others. They support (or at least acquiesce to) reforms to introduce market prices for consumer goods and health care services. But they resist adjustments that would alter the structure of public institutions especially, we suspect, where such reforms threaten the availability of public employment.

(c) Evaluations of adjustment

Three brief observations are in order about the popularly perceived impact of SAPs in Southern Africa. First, because many citizens are unaware of their government's macro-economic strategy, they cannot offer a meaningful assessment of its effects. They thereby find themselves excluded from national policy debates about the appropriate roles for markets and the state in economic development. Second, negative evaluations of economic structural adjustment greatly outweigh positive evaluations in every country, being twice as likely in South Africa and more than ten times as likely in Zimbabwe. Third, adverse convictions prevail whether people are asked about effects on themselves or on others. Since these responses are virtually indistinguishable, we suppose that people project from their own experiences to infer disequalizing societal consequences.[1] Either way, people consistently say that adjustment has made lives worse (or hurt most people) (see Table 9).

Table 9. Impact of Adjustment, Southern Africa 1999–2000

	Malawi	Zambia	Zimbabwe	S.Africa
The Structural Adjustment Program has hurt most people and only benefited a minority.	32	31	77	7
The Structural Adjustment Program has helped most people; only a minority have suffered.	11	8	7	4
Don't know/Not applicable.	57	61	16	89

(d) Explaining support for economic reform

We end by probing for reasons why people support or oppose market liberalization. As a first step, we construct an additive *index of support for economic reforms*, which is a simple count of the number of policies within the reform program that people say they support.[2] Overall, average support across all four components is highest in South Africa and Zimbabwe (49%) and lowest in Malawi and Namibia (36%) (see

---

1. Pearson's correlation = .990, sig. = .000.
2. All those who said they did not know, or agreed with neither option, were added to those who preferred the non-reform option.

Table 8). However, levels of support are low overall: only 15% of Zimbabweans agree with all four policies, and just 23% of South Africans agree with three components (see Table 10). In short, popular support for an orthodox adjustment package is partial at best.

Table 10. Support for Component Policies of Economic Reform

Number of Policies Supported	Botswana	Malawi	Namibia	Zambia	Zimbabwe	Lesotho	South Africa
0	13	18	15	15	16	13	9
1	27	37	44	31	24	36	27
2	34	31	25	27	25	36	32
3	21	12	14	18	20	14	23
4	5	2	3	9	15	2	9

We then conducted a multivariate analysis to explain the index of support for economic reform using all previous predictors (see Appendix, Model G). Consistent with earlier findings, poverty plays an important role in reducing support for economic reform, though employment and housing conditions again have no independent effect. At the same time, an individual's exposure to information, plus the liberality of resultant economic values, also increase support for adjustment. Most importantly, cross-national and racial differences again stand out. White respondents are more supportive of market-conforming reforms than blacks. And, once other factors are controlled, Zimbabweans, Zambians and Batswana are more supportive of the orthodox reform package than South Africans, while Malawians and Namibians are less so.

Deciphering 'Race' and 'Country'

In short, racial and national differences are consistently evident in mass economic attitudes in the Southern Africa region. In South Africa, for example, whites are much more likely than blacks to support the components of the standard economic reform package. These groups part company on user fees for medical services (81% versus 58%), the downsizing of the civil service (77% versus 40%), and the privatization of public corporations (88% versus 37%). Across the region, such chasms of opinion survive controls for all other considerations, including education and media use. And, along with country effects, racial group membership is so strong as to wash out rational calculations of support for reform based on popular evaluations of economic performance (see Model G). Indeed, differences across nationalities and social groups are generally greater than attitudinal differences among individuals (see all Models).

To show that races and nationalities hold singular opinions, however, is to beg the question of "why". Are there material interests that lie behind these social constructs? We attempt to decipher "race" and "country" in Model H, by replacing dummy variables with aggregate indicators of economic conditions.

Take "race". We calculated mean unemployment rates for each racial group from Afrobarometer data (see Table 1), which show significantly higher joblessness among blacks than whites. When these group proxies are plugged into the model we find that support for economic reform declines to the extent that one's own group is unemployed. Indeed, whether or not the respondent is personally out of work actually matters much less than whether unemployment is a generic problem affecting the members of his or her community. The impact of "race" is explicable in good part by assessments of the job prospects of one's reference group. Even in a growing economy, and especially under policies of privatization and civil service retrenchment, Southern African blacks face considerable uncertainty about job opportunities. Whites are less worried that reforms will eliminate their jobs because they know that most of their friends, relatives and colleagues enjoy relative job security.

In addition, the distribution of attitudes to reform can be traced to the dissolution of settler colonial rule and the attainment of majority self-government throughout the region, most recently in South Africa. Once black majorities gain control of the state, they promote the Africanization of public employment and widen the distribution of public housing, education and health care. These gains naturally lead blacks to defend state-centred policies and institutions. Whites, by contrast, can no longer rely on discriminatory job reservation policies for privileged access to public employment or quality health care. They therefore become latter-day converts to free markets, which reward the advantages in education and training bestowed on them under the old dispensation.

We also enquire about the meaning of "country". We propose that, in good part, this concept also stands for macro-economic conditions. In Model H, we replaced country dummy variables with three indicators of national wealth, economic growth, and the size of the state, all derived from a standard statistical source.[1] This final model causes us to revise and refine our findings. All other things being equal, persons who live in wealthier countries (in a relatively poor region) or in economies that are growing (during a largely stagnant period), are more likely to stick with the policy *status quo* and to reject reform. The contrary is equally true and may be even more important: living in an especially poor country with a declining quality of life makes people more likely to support reform. In short, conditions of economic crisis

---

1. World Bank, (2001: 15, 33). National wealth was measured as GNP per capita, 1990–99; economic growth was measured as the percentage change in GDP between 1990 and 1999; and the size of the state was measured as government consumption as a percentage of GDP.

make Southern Africans more willing to take a chance on the unknown outcomes of policy adjustment.

These findings help in the interpretation of national cases. A good part of the reason South Africans and Zimbabweans appear to embrace reform more whole-heartedly than other Southern Africans (see Table 8) is because the populations of these countries contain substantial minorities of job-holding white citizens. Blacks in these countries, especially if unemployed, are much less supportive. And the deep economic crisis in Zambia – which has caused the country to drop from middle- to low-income status since independence, and output per capita and quality of life to shrink over the past decade – helps to explain why Zambians will now tolerate a larger number of economic policy experiments than their neighbours in Botswana, Malawi, and Lesotho (see Table 10).

Finally, we note that a large state – meaning an extensive scope of governmental involvement in economic activity – builds support for economic reform. Indeed, our model indicates that the size of the state has more impact on building reform constituencies than any other consideration. This effect is especially evident in Namibia and Botswana, which possess relatively capable states that are the largest in the region relative to the size of their national economies. Whether Southern Africans live in rich or poor countries, they take the state as their starting point for thinking about development strategy. Indeed, they are more likely to countenance economic reforms if an effective developmental state provides a safety net against the failure of markets.

Conclusions

Many factors will determine the prospects for economic development in Southern Africa, including the availability of investment capital, the protection of property rights, and the quality of governance. But market-oriented reforms will not be sustained if they do not win popular acceptance. And, to succeed, any development strategy will have to take into account the expressed demand by Southern Africans for the state to remain involved in economic management and social redistribution. In this respect our survey respondents offer solid popular confirmation of the emerging expert consensus that a revitalized state has a major role to play in facilitating market-based development.[1]

Popular views on structural adjustment vary widely across the region and cannot be neatly characterized as simply pro- or anti-reform. To a significant degree, Southern Africans embrace the values upon which economic liberalization is based, such as personal economic independence. At the same time, however, they assert that the state should continue to take prime responsibility for core developmental services in

---

1. Among others, see World Bank (1997), Sandbrook (2000), van de Walle (2001), and Stiglitz (2002).

the agricultural, educational and health sectors, and for creating jobs. Thus they advocate a mixed economy in which the state performs as both provider and facilitator. For example, while welcoming a loosening of controls on informal trade, people insist that the state provide the financial capital required by small-scale producers. And, although individuals want freedom to engage in self-improvement, they also expect the state to expand public employment and provide a safety net for those who cannot help themselves.

Consistent with these hybrid preferences, Southern Africans express discriminating attitudes about the component policies of orthodox economic reform programs. On one hand, they accept the need to "get prices right" by expressing willingness to pay user fees in order to raise service standards and, to some extent, to endure higher consumer prices, so long as commodities remain in plentiful supply. At the same time, however, there is a strong undercurrent of popular resistance to major institutional reforms like the privatization of public enterprises and the downsizing of the civil service. From Zambia in the north to South Africa in the south, the implementation of these policies so far has been accompanied by drastic losses of formal sector employment, losses that have been visited disproportionally on black Africans. New investments by multinational corporations and the expansion of the informal sector have been unable to offset these losses. In the absence of a large-scale, indigenous private sector that delivers permanent, well-paid jobs, economic liberalization will attract only a tentative mass constituency.

In explaining the origins of mass economic attitudes, our research points to both societal and cultural foundations. Poverty, which is widespread in the region, has a consistent and important impact, reducing liberal economic values and limiting support for reform policies. Ironically, the very material conditions that reforms are intended to ameliorate are themselves important obstacles to developing mass constituencies for reform. Certain cultural attributes of modernization also shape economic worldviews. Individuals who are interested in political and economic affairs, who are self-motivated and upwardly mobile, and who attend schools and absorb news from the mass media, are primed to become the agents of economic liberalization. Somewhat surprisingly, we find little evidence that citizens adopt policy preferences on the basis of rational choice. The Southern African data suggest that people support or oppose reform independently of how they perceive the economic performance of their households, the nation, or the government.

Instead we think that economic attitudes derive primarily from the region's history of settler colonialism. This institutional legacy combined industrial market development with labor migration on a regional scale. European settlers made use of a large state apparatus to recruit and manage a reliable supply of migrant African labor and to distribute the benefits of economic growth to themselves. It is therefore unsurprising that, in the contemporary period, attitudes to economic reform still break down along racial and national lines, or that these identities should be underpinned by fundamental conflicts of economic interest. Nor is it surprising that, once blacks gain control of the state machinery, they prefer to use its instrumentalities to redress economic inequalities.

A racially polarized distribution of policy preferences, however, poses a challenge for the future acceptability of a market-based development strategy. Will the existence of a core constituency for market reform among white property owners serve as a model for the development of the economies of Southern African as a whole? Or will the market-based strategy become politically discredited because it is perceived as perpetuating a system that has led to deep social inequality based on race? As the current dispute over private land ownership in Zimbabwe attests, it is in the resolution of this tension that the future economic prospects of the region in large part depend.

References

Bekker, I. (ed.) (1994), *The strategic silence: Gender and economic policy.* Zed Books, London.

Bratton M. and C. Landsberg (2000), "South Africa", in S. Forman and S. Patrick (Eds), *Good intentions: Pledges of aid for post-conflict recovery,* pp. 268–289. Boulder: Lynne Rienner.

Dashwood H. (2000), *The political economy of transformation.* Toronto: University of Toronto Press.

Dercon, S. (2000), "Income risk, coping strategies and safety nets", *Centre for the Study of African Economies, Working Paper 2000–26.* Oxford: University of Oxford.

Domingo, E. (1995), "Perceptions and reactions to the implementation of structural adjustment in Benin", in Mkandawire, & Olukoshi, 1995.

Elster, J. (1993,) "The necessity and impossibility of simultaneous economic and political reform", in D. Greenberg (Ed.) *Constitutional democracy: Transitions in the contemporary world,* pp. 268–79. New York: Oxford University Press.

Gurr, T.R. (1970), *Why men rebel.* Princeton: Princeton University Press.

Harrison, L. and S. Huntington (2000), Editors, *Culture matters: How values shape human progress.* New York: Basic Books.

Jenkins, C. and J. Knight (2002), *The economic decline of Zimbabwe: Neither growth nor equity.* New York: Palgrave.

Kinder, D. and B. Kiewet (1981), "Sociotropic politics: the American case", *British Journal of Political Science* 11 3 (1981), pp. 129–161.

Mkandawire, T. and A. Olukoshi (eds), (1995), *Between liberalization and oppression: The politics of structural adjustment in Africa.* Dakar: CODESRIA.

Mkandawire, T. and C. Soludo (1999), *Our continent, our future: African perspectives on structural adjustment.* Trenton, NJ.:Africa World Press.

Mlambo A.S. (1997), *The economic structural adjustment program: The case of Zimbabwe, 1990–1995.* Harare: University of Zimbabwe Publications.

Natrass, N. and J. Seekings (2001), "Democracy and distribution in highly unequal economies", *Journal of Modern African Studies* 39, 3, pp. 471–498.

North, D. (1990), *Institutions, institutional change, and economic performance.* New York: Cambridge University Press.

Nyerere, J. (1968), *Ujamaa: The basis of African socialism,* London: Oxford University Press.

O'Donnell, G. (1999), *Do economists really know best?*, in L. Diamond and M. Plattner (Eds), *The global resurgence of democracy* (2nd ed.), Baltimore, MD.:Johns Hopkins University.

Przeworski, A. (1996), "Public support for economic reforms in Poland", *Comparative Political Studies* 29 5, pp. 520–543.

Republic of South Africa (1995), *Key indicators of poverty.* Pretoria: Reconstruction and Development Program.

Republic of South Africa (1996), *Growth, employment and redistribution: a macroeconomic strategy.* Pretoria: Department of Finance.

Rose, R. (1998), "Getting things done with social capital new Russia barometer VII", *Studies in public policy no. 303.* Glasgow: Center for the Study of Public Policy, University of Strathclyde.

Rose, R., and C. Haerpfer (1998), "New democracies barometer V: a 12 nation survey", *Studies in public policy,* no. 306, Glasgow: Center for the Study of Public Policy, University of Strathclyde.

Sahn D., et al. (1997), *Structural adjustment reconsidered: Economic policy and poverty in Africa.* New York: Cambridge University Press.

Sandbrook, R. (2000), *Closing the circle: Democratization and development in Africa.* London: Zed Books.

Sarrasin, B. (1999), *Ajustement structurel et lutte contre la pauvreté en Afrique: La Banque mondiale face à la critique.* Paris: Harmattan.

Shiller, R., et al. (1991), "Popular attitudes to free markets: the Soviet Union and the United States compared", *The American Economic Review* 81 3, pp. 385–400. Abstract-EconLit.

Statistics South Africa (2000), *Labour force survey* (September). Pretoria: Statistics SA.

Stavrou, S., 2000, "Infrastructural services", in J. May, (Ed.) *Poverty and inequality in South Africa.* Cape Town/London: David Philip Publishers/Zed Books.

Stiglitz, J. (2002), *Globalization and its discontents.* London: Norton.

Tati, G. (1995), "Congo: social reactions and the political stakes in the dynamics of structural adjustment", in T. Mkandawire, & A. Olukoshi (Eds), pp. 345–373.

Vambe, M.T. (2000), "Popular songs and social realities in post-independence Zimbabwe", *African Studies Review* 43 2 , pp. 73–86.

van de Walle, N. (2001), *African economies and the politics of permanent crisis.* New York: Cambridge University Press.

Walton J., and D. Seddon (1994), *Free markets and food riots: The politics of global adjustment.* London: Blackwell.

Whitefield S. and G. Evans (1999), "Political culture and rational choice: explaining responses to transition in the Czech Republic and Slovakia" *British Journal of Political Science* 29 2 , pp. 129–155.

World Bank (1981), *Accelerated development in sub-Saharan Africa: An agenda for Africa.* Washington DC.: World Bank.

World Bank (1994), *Adjustment in Africa: Reforms, results and the road ahead.* New York: Oxford University Press.

World Bank (1997), *World Development report, 1997: The state in a changing world.* New York: Oxford University Press.

World Bank (2000), *Can Africa claim the 21st century?* Washington DC.: World Bank.

World Bank (2001), *African development indicators, 2001.* Washington, DC.: WorldBank.

Appendix

The Afrobarometer

The Afrobarometer is a comparative series of national public attitude surveys on democracy, markets and civil society in Africa. It is jointly managed by the Institute for Democracy in South Africa (IDASA), the Ghana Center for Democratic Development (CDD), and Michigan State University (MSU). Research institutions in each country implement national surveys. The sample sizes for each country are as follows: Botswana = 1200, Lesotho = 1177, Malawi = 1208, Namibia = 1183, South Africa = 2200, Zambia = 1200, and Zimbabwe = 1200. The margin of sampling error is plus or minus 3 percentage points (2.2 per cent in South Africa). Samples were designed using a multi-stage, stratified, area cluster approach. Random selection methods were used at each stage, with probability proportional to population size. Sampling frames were constructed from the most up-to-date census figures or projections available, and thereafter from census maps, systematic walk patterns, and project-generated lists of household members. With the exception of South Africa (where racial minorities were over-sampled and weighted), each country sample was self-weighted and representative of national characteristics on key socio-economic indicators (gender, age, region). Research was supported by the United States Agency for International Development's Regional Center for Southern Africa. For further information, see www.afrobarometer.org.

Multivariate Regression Models

Dependent Variables:
Model A: Poverty
Model B: Economic Satisfaction
Model C: Relative Deprivation
Model D: Approval of Government Economic Management
Model E: Personal Economic Independence
Model F: Favor Private Provision of Development Services
Models G and H: Support for Economic Reform

	Model A	Model B	Model C	Model D	Model E	Model F	Model G	Model H
Constant (b)	2.918	3.097	2.967	2.723	1.294	1.306	1.015	2.074
LIVING CONDITIONS								
Poverty	.	-13***	.24***	-.18***	-.12***	-.05***	-.08***	-.09***
Employment	-.10***	.00	-.03**	-.03**	.01	.02	.03*	.03
Improved House	.	.01	-.02	-.02	.00	.01	-.01	.01
ECONOMIC EVALUATIONS								
Economic Satisfaction	.	.	.	.	.04*	.03	.01	-.00
Relative Deprivation	.	.	.	.	-.05**	-.00	-.02	-.01
Govt. Econ. Management	.	.	.	.	.05**	.02	.01	.02
ECONOMIC VALUES								
Risk Acceptance	.	.	.	.	-.06***	.03*	.06***	.09***
Value Econ. Independence	.	.	.	.	.	.	.07***	.07***
Favor Private Provision	.	.	.	.	.	.	.09***	.08***
POLITICAL ATTITUDES								
Political Interest	.	-.02	-.03	.02	.06***	.01	.01	.00
Political Efficacy	.	.	.	.	.03	.03	.02	.04*
Trust in Government	.	.	.	.	-.01	-.03	-01	-.05*
Interpersonal Trust	.	.	.	.	.02	-.00	-.03	-.04*

	Model A	Moel B	Model C	Model D	Model E	Model F	Model G	Model H
SOCIO-DEMOGRAPHICS								
Rural/Urban	-.14***	-.02	.01	-.04*	.02	.00	.02	.03
Education	-.19***	-.02	-.03*	-.06***	.07***	.12***	.04*	.08***
News Media Use	.	.01	-.06***	.05**	.07***	.09***	13***	.11***
Age	.02	-.06***	-.04***	-.05***	.00	-00	-.01	.02
Gender	.02	.01	.00	.02	-.00	.03*	.01	.01
RACE								
Asian	-11***	-.10***	.04***	-.15***	-.01	-.08***	.03*	
Coloured	-14***	-.03*	.02	-.06***	.01	-.01	.03*	
White	-17***	-.15***	.09***	-.18***	.09***	.00	.15***	
Race Group Unemployment	.	.	.	.	.	.	.	-16***
COUNTRY								
Botswana	-17***	.11***	.02	.19***	.05**	.00	.06***	
Lesotho	-.05***	-.05***	.05***	.02	.06***	.04*	.04*	
Malawi	-.04***	-.03	-.07***	-.01	.30***	.24***	-.05*	
Namibia	.06***	.25***	-.14***	.22***	.10***	.07***	-.02	
Zambia	.16***	-.03*	-.06***	.04**	.07***	.00	.07***	
Zimbabwe	.08***	-.34***	.16***	-.15***	-.02	.14***	.12***	
Macro-Economic Conditions								
National Wealth	.	.	.	.	.	.	.	-11***
Economic Growth	.	.	.	.	.	.	.	-.06***
Size of State	.	.	.	.	.	.	.	.06***
N	8215	6602	7530	6548	4498	4466	4185	4185
ADJUSTED R SQUARED	.27	.26	.15	.19	.15	.09	.15	.16
S.E. of Regression	.6941	.9074	1.0567	.6618	.9623	.3675	1.0257	1.0244

Notes to Appendix

Figures for each independent variable are standardized regression coefficients
i.e. Betas (except constants, which are unstandardized b's).
*** statistical significance =< .001.
** statistical significance =< .01.
* statistical significance =<.05.
 If cells contain a dot (.), the variable was excluded from the regression model.

5. Economic Integration Efforts in Southern Africa

Mats Lundahl and Lennart Petersson[1]

Since the middle of the 1970s, the aggregate economic performance of sub-Saharan Africa has fallen below that of other developing areas. Overall GDP growth has decelerated, and since 1980, aggregate GDP per capita has decreased by almost 1 per cent per annum (Collier and Gunning, 1999: 3, Petersson, 2001: 249). As a result, sub-Saharan Africa is the region with the lowest average income in the world. The explanations for this performance differ. Some argue that the main cause of slow growth is found in factors related to foreign trade policy (Collier and Gunning, 1999: 6). Tariffs were higher and quantitative trade restrictions more extensive in Africa than elsewhere, due to the use of import substitution, adopted partly for lack of other sources of tax revenue. This, together with overvalued exchange rates, resulted in an anti-export bias, which has contributed to the halving of the share of sub-Saharan Africa in world exports since 1970 (Svedberg, 1999: 13, WTO, 1998: 55, Ng and Yeats 2000: Table 3.2).

A rival explanation of low growth centres on the unfavourable structure of production and trade. Few countries in sub-Saharan Africa have succeeded in increasing manufactured exports, and the domination of one or a few primary products in exports may have contributed to volatile and deteriorating terms of trade. Furthermore, it is argued that such geographic and demographic characteristics as poor soil quality, low population density and small populations may predispose sub-Saharan Africa to slow growth (Collier and Gunning, 1999: 7–10). Since the 1980s, the slow growth rate has also been attributed to domestic economic policies that have created financial imbalances and an unstable macroeconomic environment.

During the past four decades various attempts have been made to increase the economic integration of Africa south of the Sahara, with a view to promoting growth and expanding the industrial base. Although most integration arrangements have so far failed, there was a renewed interest in regional issues in the 1990s. This was the case especially in southern Africa, the focus of this chapter, where major developments reinforced the attention given to integration. The most prominent regional event was the transition to democracy in South Africa and the end of the destabilization policy pursued by the previous minority government of that country. The reincorporation of Africa's largest market and most sophisticated economy into

1. Financial support from the Swedish International Development Cooperation Agency (Sida) is gratefully acknowledged. Thanks are due to Arne Bigsten, Steven Friedman, Kerstin Sahlin-Andersson and Göran Therborn for constructive criticism.

the world economy has created optimistic expectations of a more rewarding integration of the southern African region.

Another matter of interest in the discussion on economic integration is the effect of regionalism and globalization on development, particularly in the low-income countries of sub-Saharan Africa. Rapid changes in technology have brought about changes in the international division of labor and have significantly altered the competitive environment. It can be argued that the low level of processing, the poor technology base and the fragmented markets do not yet make it meaningful for the countries of southern Africa to participate in a multilateral free trade system. Thus, regional integration is seen as a response to the threat of marginalization and to the emergence of trading blocs in other parts of the world (Lipalile, 2001: 305). The hope is that economic integration will enable the countries in the region to strengthen their voice in world affairs, and to merge their fragmented markets into a regional market capable of competing directly with other, already established, regional markets. The successful development of what is sometimes referred to as 'open regionalism', in contrast to closed, import-substituting, regionalism, is seen as a stepping stone towards integration into the global system, i.e. as an instrument of trade liberalization.

A third important factor in the context of regional integration is the widespread implementation of structural adjustment programs, supported by the IMF and the World Bank, as well as various domestic adjustment and reform attempts (Mistry, 1996). This is likely to have an effect on regional integration because inconsistencies between macroeconomic policies and trade regimes can undermine both regional and unilateral trade liberalization (Harvey, 1999, IMF, 2000: 24–29, 34–35, Jenkins, Leape and Thomas, 2000: 2–12). The argument is that a credible macroeconomic stabilization policy is crucial for the formation of an economic region capable of attracting foreign investment and competing with other regions in the world market. In this approach, the concept of 'economic region' is related to harmonization of national economic policies (policy integration) and macroeconomic convergence.

In the present chapter, the region of southern Africa refers to the fourteen members of the Southern African Development Community (SADC): Angola, Botswana, the Democratic Republic of Congo, Lesotho, Malawi, Mauritius, Mozambique, Namibia, the Seychelles, South Africa, Swaziland, Tanzania, Zambia and Zimbabwe. We will analyze the prospects for mutually advantageous economic integration between these countries, by identifying those underlying characteristics of their economies that make them more or less likely to benefit from market integration. This includes the conditions for the convergence of macroeconomic policies. The main analysis will be restricted to the eleven member countries of the SADC Free Trade Area (SADC FTA) (excluding Angola, the Democratic Republic of Congo and the Seychelles). First the rationale of economic integration for the small developing countries of southern Africa will be dealt with. An analysis of trade policies in the 1990s and the present institutions for integration in the region follows. Third, a number of geographic and demographic characteristics of the region as well as various industrial and trade patterns are reviewed in order to shed some light on the prospects of integrating the small fragmented markets into a larger regional one. Finally, the issue of regional harmonization of macroeconomic policy and convergence of key macroeconomic variables is discussed.

The Rationale of Integration

The orthodox theory of integration (Viner, 1950), constructed with developed countries in mind, is concerned with the gains that may be derived from changes in the existing pattern of production and trade. Full employment and given factor endowments are assumed. In markets characterized by perfect competition, the gains from integration are derived from enhanced efficiency in production made possible by increased specialization and trade in accordance with comparative advantage, with some sectors expanding and others contracting (Lundahl and Petersson, 1991: Chapter 6, Robson, 1998: Chapter 2). The analyses of the impact of regional integration on resource allocation and welfare are usually based on Viner's distinction between the replacement of domestic production by cheaper imports from partner countries (trade creation) and the replacement of imports from non-member countries by imports from higher-cost member countries (trade diversion). In the low-income countries of southern Africa, however, it is often unemployment and underutilization of resources rather than reallocation of employed resources that are the relevant targets for integration. The expansion of the industrial base is regarded as the driving force of rapid economic development. In this context, the dynamic effects of a larger regional market are seen to provide an opportunity to diversify and stimulate growth by exploiting economies of scale and encouraging foreign investment and technological progress (Lundahl and Petersson, 1991: Chapter 7).

Past import substitution policies in southern Africa were largely based on the infant industry argument: even though a developing country may have a potential comparative advantage in certain products, temporary measures are needed to get industrialization started. Thus, several nations attempted to accelerate development by limiting their imports of manufactured goods to foster a manufacturing sector serving the domestic markets. When these markets proved too small, the formation of regional markets was seen as a way out – as a way to achieve collective import substitution that lowered the cost that each individual country would face on its own. The enlarged regional market may also serve as a training ground for exporting elsewhere (McCarthy, 1996: 215), for infant export activities that need to develop quality control, marketing techniques and other prerequisites for later success in international markets.

In the modern approach to infant industries the focus is on external economies of scale, i.e. the cost per unit depends on the size of the industry but not necessarily on the size of any single firm. This means that the efficiency of the industrial sectors of regions and countries increases with the total size of production, and that production must reach a 'critical mass' for development to take off (Ottaviano and Puga, 1998). The argument is that many industries require the use of specialized equipment or support services, and that a small industrial sector does not provide a market for these services that is large enough to keep the suppliers in business. Large markets also support the local production of intermediate goods (forward linkages), increasing quality and/or lowering costs for downstream producers. In the labor market there may be gains from pooling. Firms in a large regional market benefit from readily available labor skills, and hence from locating where other firms have already trained a pool of skilled labor.

External economies create incentives for firms to locate close to each other. This supports a regional concentration of production, as may internal economies of scale. Thus, regional integration that results in expansion of industrial production may be advantageous for the most advanced industrial producer among developing countries, because the reduction of trading costs makes it easier to supply consumers from just a few locations. This is likely to occur if manufacturing as a whole accounts for just a small share of the economy, if linkages are broad, across many sectors, and the basic infrastructure in telecommunications, the access to financial markets and other business services are initially weakly developed and unevenly spread (Venables, 1999: 17–18). One possibility, however, is that particular sectors become more spatially concentrated, i.e. relatively small sectors cluster in different specialized locations.

Since industrialization is a primary concern, a crucial issue for southern Africa is how the formation of the SADC Free Trade Area will affect the distribution of activities between member countries. Will the gains and losses be equally divided between the member countries, or will some gain production while others lose it? This issue can be analyzed by identifying the factors likely to promote trade creation and trade diversion. With respect to the objective of increasing manufacturing production for all participating countries, regardless of whether it is due to trade creation or trade diversion, the essential conditions for mutually beneficial trade integration are that prospective partners have similar industry and trade structures and similar production costs. These conditions maximize the likelihood that *all* partners can retain and expand at least some manufacturing activity in which they have a comparative advantage vis-à-vis the rest of the group (Foroutan, 1993: 255–58).

Another important factor both for the welfare effects of integration and for the location of expanding production and intra-regional trade is the level of tariffs. The higher the pre-union tariffs on goods in which there will be trade creation, the larger will be the gains. In a free trade area, the members can reduce the losses from trade diversion by introducing low tariffs towards the outside world. By the same token, the likelihood of a skewed regional distribution of production increases when there are large differences in external tariffs among members. Countries with high external tariffs that indicate low international competitiveness, in a free trade area may replace imports from non-member countries by imports from higher-cost member countries. This may favour the more advanced members of a free trade area, because for the least developed countries, tariff revenue is likely to be an important source of income which they cannot forgo.

Trade Policy and Institutions of Integration in Southern Africa

The pattern of trade restrictions, both between member countries and vis-à-vis the rest of the world, is a key characteristic of an integrated economic region. It provides a basis for predicting who gains and who loses. According to the theory of integration, the gains from expanding intra-regional exports may favour the countries with the lowest tariffs at the time of establishing a free trade area, making them gain both from trade creation and trade diversion. Therefore, we will open the analysis with a look at trade policy in the 1990s and the level of protection of the fourteen SADC countries at the end of the decade. This is followed by a presentation of the major economic groupings in southern Africa.

Trade policies in the 1990s

In the early 1990s high tariff and non-tariff trade barriers characterized most of the fourteen countries in southern Africa (IMF, 2000: 6, Jenkins and Thomas, 2000: 27–40, Mistry, 1996: 218). Using an indicator of the restrictiveness of the trading system based on both tariff and non-tariff barriers (see note to Table 1), on a scale from 0 to 10, where 10 indicates the most restrictive regime, all but three of the fourteen SADC countries scored the highest mark in 1990. During the following decade, however, most of them made significant progress in opening their economies to external competition through trade and exchange rate liberalization (Table 1). In many countries the IMF and the World Bank supported the liberalization in the context of structural adjustment programs, easing the external constraints by large grants and concessional aid flows. The trade policy of the 1980s was reversed, and trade regimes converged towards those of the rest of the world. Yet, the trade system in southern Africa remained more restricted than that of other regions (IMF, 2000: Table 3.4). Levels of protection continued to be high in Angola, the Seychelles and Zimbabwe, and Mauritius and Tanzania achieved only moderate liberalization.

The trade reforms included a substantial reduction of maximum and average import tariffs, in particular in the Seychelles, Zambia and SACU, which comprises South Africa, Botswana, Lesotho, Namibia and Swaziland. For eastern and southern Africa as a whole, the IMF estimates that the average most favored nation import tariffs came down from 35 to 15%. In the reforming countries, the maximum tariffs, which in many cases exceeded 100% at the beginning of the decade, were reduced to 25–40% (IMF, 2000: 10–11). In addition, most of the reformers simplified their complex protection systems (characterized by a large number of tariff bands, a wide spread of tariff rates, specific rates, variable duties and charges etc.), by reducing the number of non-zero rates to less than six (Belli et al., 1993: 1–3, IMF, 2000: 11). Excepting cases where health, environment and security considerations called for protection, there was a significant reduction of the substantial restrictive non-tariff barriers prevailing at the beginning of the 1990s, such as import and export quotas, import bans and state trading. At the same time, however, the use of anti-dumping measures, particularly in the SACU area, and safeguard measures received greater emphasis in the region.

Table 1. Measures of Trade Restriction 1998 and Changes in Trade Policies during the 1990s

	Trade restric. index[a] (TRI) 1998	Change in TRI in the 1990s	Average import tariff 1998	Change in average import tariff	Non-tariff barriers 1998	Exchange controls 2000
Angola	10	0	24	0	Pervasive	Substantial
Botswana	4	-6	15	-30	Few	None
Congo, Dem. Rep. of	4	-5	17	-3	Substantial	Substantial
Lesotho	4	-6	15	-30	Few	Few
Malawi	4	-3	12	-6	Few	Few
Mauritius	7	-3	19	-15	Substantial	None
Mozambique	2	-5	10	-9	None	Few
Namibia	4	-6	15	-30	Few	Few
Seychelles	10	0	38	-47	Pervasive	None
South Africa	4	-6	15	-30	Few	Few
Swaziland	4	-6	15	-30	Few	Few
Tanzania	6	-4	20	-5	Few	None
Zambia	2	-8	14	-23	None	None
Zimbabwe	9	-1	32	2	Substantial	Substantial

a.   Average indicator of trade restrictiveness developed by the International Monetary Fund on a scale from 0 to 10, where 10 indicates the most restrictive regime. The index is based on many factors, including the minimum and maximum tariff rates, the number of tariff bands, the allocation of individual items to each band, any other duties and charges, and the extent of exemptions from customs duties. Export tariffs are explicitly taken into account, and if the trade taxes of a country exceed 35 per cent, a 10 rating is accorded irrespective of the non-tariff barriers regime (IMF 2000: Appendix I).

Sources: IMF, 2000, Table 3.1, Table 3.2, Table 3.3, World Economic Forum, 2000: 108, 115, 121, 128, 135, 148, 155, 169, 176, 182, 187, 194.

There have, however, been policy reversals in the liberalization process, putting the credibility of the trade reforms in doubt. The countries that have seen partial policy reversals are Angola, the Seychelles, Zimbabwe, Tanzania, Malawi and Zambia (here ranked in descending order according to the level of restrictions in 1998). Liberalization has taken place mainly on a unilateral basis. Most of the countries, with the exception of the SACU nations, agreed to fix an upper bound only on a small number of tariffs during the multilateral Uruguay Round. Furthermore (also in the SACU countries), the bounds were put at very high levels, well above the rates that applied in practice. This means that it is possible to reverse the trade liberalization without violating any obligations under the WTO agreement.

With the exception of Angola, whose currency is not convertible, all the countries in the region liberalized their exchange rate regimes substantially (IMF, 2000: 12, World Economic Forum, 2000: 108–194). However, various types of controls remain in most countries, and they are quite significant in the Democratic Republic of Congo and Zimbabwe (on a temporary basis). The largest country in the region, South Africa, has few restrictions on current account transactions, but there are some exchange regulations that may affect outward investments by residents. Lesotho, Namibia and Swaziland are part of the Common Monetary Area (CMA), dominated by South Africa, and exchange controls applicable to the latter country thus automatically also apply to the smaller members of the monetary area. The CMA exchange controls are gradually being relaxed to allow savers to invest their money particularly in the SADC countries but also in the rest of the world (World Economic Forum, 2000: 128, 155, 169, 176).

In conclusion, the spread of tariff rates both between sectors and across the fourteen SADC countries has narrowed significantly during the 1990s, and most of the countries have reduced non-tariff barriers and eased their exchange restrictions. This means that important steps have been taken towards the formation of an economic region vis-à-vis the rest of the world, in the spirit of open regionalism. However, for most countries the wedge between bound and applied tariffs is large, and this gives room for policy reversals that reduce the credibility of the policy. In the case of SACU, the wedge is lower than the average for the region, and since the advent of majority rule in 1994, trade liberalization has been an important part of the growth strategy of South Africa, signalling that the reforms are irreversible. The experience of the past indicates that the key to irreversible trade reforms in the region is found in the ability to maintain a stable macroeconomic environment, in particular with respect to the current account balance – an issue that we will return to below.

Institutions of integration in Southern Africa

A unique characteristic of economic integration in Africa is the multiplicity and degree of overlap – what Jagdish Bhagwati (2001: Chapter 3) has called the African spaghetti bowl. At present, there are six major arrangements in the southern African region. These are the Southern African Customs Union (SACU), the Common Monetary Area (CMA), the Regional Integration Facilitation Forum (RIFF), formerly the Cross-Border Initiative (CBI), the Common Market for Eastern and Southern Africa (COMESA), the Southern African Development Community (SADC) and the SADC Free Trade Area (SADC FTA). Since the late 1980s, all these have been in a process of transformation as they attempt to respond to the new regional and global environment. Although many of the schemes so far have failed to be implemented or to deliver significant benefits, the shortcomings have not deterred the governments from going ahead with much more advanced arrangements. Thus, it is easy to agree with Robson's (1997: 348) description of integration in sub-Saharan Africa:

> 'Reculer pour mieux sauter' is not a dictum that seems to carry much weight among African governments involved in regional integration. On the contrary, if a certain level of integration cannot be made to work, the reaction of policy makers has typically been to embark on something more elaborate, more advanced and more demanding in terms of administrative requirements and political commitment.

It appears that the extraordinary economic vulnerability and fragility in southern Africa (and in the whole of the sub-Saharan region), explains much of the eagerness to use integration to overcome domestic constraints. For decades, there has been a remarkable degree of consensus with respect to the desirability of cooperation and regional integration as a road to development, and with respect to the principle that the response to failure should be more, and not less, integration.

Table 2 shows the country membership of the various groupings. The origins of SACU date back to the end of the nineteenth century (Lundahl and Petersson, 1991: Chapter 4). The present agreement came into force in 1969 following the independence of Botswana, Lesotho and Swaziland, and on independence in 1990, Namibia became a member as well (Ibid., Chapter 5). SACU is widely regarded as the most effectively functioning trade agreement in Africa. Commodity and factor markets are well integrated, and there are common external tariffs and excise taxes which are paid into a common revenue pool. The revenue is then shared by a formula according to which the BLNS countries make a disproportionate gain compared to their share of total union imports. The smaller countries allegedly receive compenzation

Table 2. Southern African Membership in Regional Groupings 2001

Country	SACU	CMA	CBI	COMESA	SADC	SADC FTA
Angola					#	
Botswana	#				#	#
Congo, Dem. Rep. of					#	
Lesotho	#	#			#	#
Malawi			#	#	#	#
Mauritius			#	#	#	#
Mozambique				#	#	#
Namibia	#	#	#	#	#	#
Seychelles			#	#	#	
South Africa	#	#			#	#
Swaziland	#	#	#	#	#	#
Tanzania			#		#	#
Zambia			#	#	#	#
Zimbabwe			#	#	#	#

Sources: Holden, (1998), Table 1, IMF, (2000), p. 2, Lee, (2001), p. 270.

for adverse effects of the union: the price-raising effects of restrictions designed primarily to protect South African industries, the loss of fiscal discretion and the natural tendency towards concentration of industrial development to areas which are already industrially advanced, all of which were located in South Africa at the time of signing the agreement. Since 1995 the agreement has been under renegotiation. There are still issues to be settled, but it appears that the negotiations have centred on the continuation of SACU. Although it is difficult to predict the outcome of a new agreement, it is quite certain that the revenue accruing to the BLNS countries will decline, but also that they will have a say in tariff and other trade policy issues.

For most of SACU's history, the member countries used a common currency, that of South Africa (Ibid., Chapter 9). Currently, Lesotho, Namibia and Swaziland issue their own currencies, but each national currency is pegged at par with the South African rand, which is allowed to circulate legally alongside each national currency. The relatively free flow of money and goods between the four countries, which are members of both SACU and the CMA, means convergence of monetary policy and indirect taxation, and hence similar inflation rates.

Eight countries participate in what used to be known as the Cross-Border Initiative (CBI) which encourages a 'fast track' to trade liberalization. The CBI originally sought to establish a free trade area among the participating countries and a harmonized external tariff by 1998. The harmonization was intended to allow for some flexibility in the tariff setting for individual countries in the short to medium term, in a process heading towards a common external tariff (Maasdorp, 1998: 91). Outcomes have fallen significantly short of the targets, but the CBI represents an interesting approach to open regionalism, combining unilateral trade liberalization with a low common external tariff with eventual free intra-regional trade. In May 2000, the CBI changed its name to the Regional Integration Facilitation Forum (RIFF). Activities were refocused on investment facilitation, simplifying investment procedures with the objective of establishing a one-stop investment approval authority. Furthermore, the agenda has been broadened to include other issues related to regional macroeconomic developments and cooperation (IMF, 2000: 17).

The Preferential Trade Area of Eastern and Southern African States (PTA) was founded in 1981 and came into force in 1983. It was intended to be the major vehicle for the promotion of trade integration by reducing customs duties and non-tariff barriers between participating countries, and the idea was to eliminate all tariffs on intra-PTA trade by the year 2000. In order to further encourage trade between members, several new institutions were introduced, such as the PTA Clearing House, as a step towards a monetary and payment zone, and the PTA Bank for Trade and Development, to promote economic and social development (Söderbaum, 1996: 41–42). The number of regional programs and sectors increased over time, but the success of the PTA was very limited. Finally, in 1990 the PTA adopted a monetary harmonization program aimed at a monetary union by 2020 (Holden, 1998: 462).

In December 1994, the PTA was transformed into what is now known as the Common Market for Eastern and Southern Africa (COMESA): eighteen countries in eastern and southern Africa plus Djibouti, Egypt and the Sudan (Holden, 1998: 461–63, IMF, 2000: 17, Söderbaum, 1996: 40–45). COMESA intended to remove the organizational weakness of the PTA, strengthening the existing institutions and setting up some new ones. The failure to create a free trade area by the year 2000 has not deterred the organization from formulating even more ambitious goals. The current aim of COMESA is to establish a customs union by 2004, with a common external tariff and a small number of tariff bands (IMF, 2000: 17).

The Southern African Development Coordination Conference (SADCC) was founded in 1980 by five so-called frontline states. It had a basically political objective: to coordinate measures that would reduce economic dependency, particularly on South Africa. The principal function of SADCC was to coordinate the allocation of a great number of projects in various sectors, mainly in transport and communications. In 1992, SADCC was transformed into the Southern African Development Community (SADC) with much more ambitious objectives than those of its predecessor, seeking to obtain cooperation in most sectors of the economy with sector responsibility distributed among the individual member countries. South Africa joined in 1994, strengthening the organization, Mauritius followed suit in 1995, and the Democratic Republic of Congo and the Seychelles in 1997. South Africa was given the responsibility for the SADC Finance and Investment Sector Coordinating Unit (FISCU), that was to prepare cooperation in investment, macroeconomic convergence, development finance, and the activities of the region's central banks (World Economic Forum, 2000: 21).

In 1997 eleven SADC members including South Africa agreed to a Trade Protocol drafted in 1996 that aimed at phasing in a free trade area over a period of eight years, and in 1998 they agreed to expedite the negotiation process (Lee, 2001: 254). The objective was to increase the diversification and industrialization of the region and to ensure efficient production within SADC, in a way that reflected the current and dynamic comparative advantage of its members (SADC, 1996: Article 2). This was to be achieved through further liberalization of intra-regional trade on the basis of fair, mutually equitable and beneficial trade arrangements as well as through an improved climate for domestic, cross-border and foreign investments. The negotiation of tariff reduction was slow, but in early 2000 a trade accord was finally reached.

The date for the implementation of an eleven-nation free trade area (SADC11) was set for 1 September 2000[1] (IMF, 2000: 17–18). There are large differences in

---

1. Three SADC member states, Angola, the Democratic Republic of Congo and the Seychelles, were not to take part in the early stage of the project.

external tariffs across SADC countries and no plans for a common external tariff. In order to limit trade deflection – the redirection of imports through the country with the lowest tariff for the purpose of exploiting the tariff differential – the member states have agreed to develop product-specific rules of origin for all traded goods (Lee, 2001: 264).

A complication for the integration process in southern Africa is the overlapping membership in regional economic organizations. SACU is the only customs union in the region, but other organizations may consider the introduction of a common external tariff that may differ from that of SACU. If so, it is not clear which external tariff system individual countries participating in both schemes will follow. Furthermore, different free trade areas may have different rules of origin, and this, in turn, complicates marketing and production decisions for companies, and creates onerous internal procedures to establish the origin of goods coming from different groups of countries. The question is whether market integration can be successfully implemented under these circumstances. In addition, according to the SADC Protocol on Trade, SADC member states are allowed both to maintain existing bilateral trading agreements and to conclude new ones (Lee, 2001: 271). Finally, there are large administrative and political costs and distractions stemming from multiple initiatives and overlapping memberships. Consequently, there is an urgent need to rationalize the initiatives.

Economic Characteristics and Trade Patterns of SADC Countries

It is usually argued that it is easier to integrate countries with similar economic characteristics and development levels, because this reduces the adjustment costs of trade expansion and increases the likelihood of mutual benefits. Furthermore, geographic and demographic characteristics of a region, such as supply of natural resources, population density, size and distribution of total population, surface area, GDP and industrial sector production, are all important determinants of the success or failure of economic performance (Collier and Gunning, 1999: 7–10).

The 9.1 million square kilometres of surface area of the fourteen SADC countries cover almost a third of Africa's land mass (about the size of the U.S.). In 1999, these countries had a population of 195 million (somewhat less than Indonesia) and a combined GDP of US$ 187 billion (about as much as Denmark) (World Bank 2001b: Tables 1-1, 2-5). However, the SADC countries vary considerably in land area, population and in population density. The three largest countries by land area (Democratic Republic of Congo, Angola and South Africa) cover no less than half of the total surface area and house about half of the SADC population. The four smallest (Seychelles, Mauritius, Swaziland and Lesotho) together cover about half a per cent of the land mass and 2% of the population. The large total land area of the region means that there are significant variations in climatic conditions, in forest cover and availability of arable land (BMR, 1997: 38, World Bank, 2001b: Tables 1-1 and 8–12).

There are large disparities among and within the SADC countries both economically and in terms of human development ratings. GNP per capita ranges from US$ 120 in the Democratic Republic of Congo to US$ 6,540 in the Seychelles (1999). Eight SADC countries are classified as low-income countries in the World Bank ranking, with a GNP per capita of less than US$ 755, and for six of the countries it was less than half of this level. The region is dominated by South Africa, which accounts for about one-fifth of the population, but for around 70% of the total GDP. The country's manufacturing production is five times larger, and the capacity in such sectors as transport, energy and financial services is greatly superior to the rest of the region. The economic structures of the SADC countries also reflect great heterogeneity. The agricultural sector plays an important role in the low-income SADC economies, but in five countries less than 10% of GDP was generated by it (World Bank, 2001a: Table 4.2). In most economies, the share of industry (including mineral extraction, construction, water and electricity) by and large coincide with the world average for low and middle-income countries and the average for sub-Saharan Africa.

The SADC countries in general are open economies. Merchandise imports and exports together account for sizeable proportions of their GDP. With the exception of Tanzania and Mozambique where trade-GDP ratios are relatively low – around 26% – the ratios of other member countries range between 36% for the Democratic Republic of Congo and 161% for Swaziland (1998). The ratio for South Africa is 42% and the average for the fourteen SADC countries is 47%. The bulk of the exports is destined for non-SADC countries in the form of primary products. In 1998, manufactures accounted for a mere 10% of the exports of southern Africa (excluding South Africa, where the figure was about one-third) (Holden, 1998: 465, World Bank, 2001b). Intra-regional trade is, however, dominated by trade in manufactures (Valentine, 1998: Table 8).

The distribution of gains and losses of preferential trade arrangements between countries depend on the existing and expected trade patterns among participants. Since the mid-1980s, the volume of intra-SADC trade has grown, and the intra-regional share of total trade has increased. From 1985 to 1996 imports supplied by the region increased from 3.1% to 6.8% of total SADC imports (Tsikata, 1999: Table 6). The aim of the SADC free trade area is to develop the manufacturing sector by improved access to the regional market. Thus, in Table 3 we report the matrix of intra-SADC manufacturing trade in the free trade area (SADC11). Because reliable trade statistics for the smaller countries of SACU are not available, the members of the customs union are treated as a group. The proportion of SADC imports supplied by the region was 10.6% in 1995–96. For the non-SACU countries, except Mauritius, the ratio was significantly higher – ranging from 62.7% to 90.1% for

Malawi, Mozambique, Zambia and Zimbabwe. For the SACU area, the intra-regional share of total imports was a tiny 1.1%.

On average, SADC is the destination for almost 18% of total SADC manufac-turing exports and significantly higher percentages are reported for Malawi, Mozambique and Zimbabwe. Consequently, for some of the participating countries, SADC is an important export market. The very divergent pattern of industrializa-tion has, however, resulted in a corresponding variability in total intra-group trade. In 1995–96, almost 85% of total intra-regional exports originated in SACU, domi-nated by South Africa, and another 11% in Zimbabwe. SACU is also the main desti-nation of non-SACU exports to the region (56%).

Table 3. Direction of Trade Matrix and Trade Imbalance Index (TII) of SADC11 for Manufactures: Average 1995–96 (1,000 US$)

Imports Exports	MWI	MRT	MOZ	SACU	TZA	ZMB	ZWE	SADC11	SADC % of total exp.
MWI	0	9	7,563	40,998	2,932	1,127	5,176	57,805	39.0
MRT	525	0	11	3,280	1,602	98	9,373	14,889	1.0
MOZ	593	0	0	9,806	127	58	7,094	17,678	37.2
SACU	196,777	180,710	549,123	0	135,784	353,559	1,183,220	2,599,173	18.7
TZA	189	647	0	1,517	0	0	1,082	3,435	1.2
ZMB	1,497	6	240	15,006	0	0	8,774	25,523	23.5
ZWE	39,378	1,985	44,979	188,123	3,967	65,402	0	343,834	34.7
SADC11	238,959	183,357	601,916	258,730	144,412	420,244	1,214,719	3,062,337	17.9
SADC % of total Import	67.4	11.9	90.1	1.1	14.4	62.7	70.6	10.6	
Regional TII[a]	-0.61	-0.85	-0.94	0.82	-0.95	-0.89	-0.56		

[a] TII is the trade imbalance index, which for each country shows the value of net trade with the SADC11 group of countries (exports minus imports) as a share of its total trade (exports plus imports) with the SADC11 group of countries.

Source: Compiled from data from Industrial Development Corporation South Africa.

Despite the growth of intra-SADC trade, the prospects for a significant expansion of trade between the member countries are not good – because most countries have small manufacturing sectors and a narrow export base. Imports from the region already constitute a large proportion of total imports for several countries, but not for the dominating economy in the region, South Africa. The dominance of South Africa (SACU) in the total trade of the region means that a substantial increase of intra-regional trade in relation to total trade must involve increased exports to that country, reducing the severe imbalance in trade between SACU and the rest of the countries. (All countries outside SACU have substantial deficits in intra-regional trade; see Table 3.) In the 1990s, the proportion of SACU imports with their origin in the non-SACU countries has, however, increased only slightly, from 0.8% in 1991 to 1.2% in 1999 (Petersson, 2002: Table 1). The reason is that scale-intensive and differentiated product groups account for the major part of South Africa's expanding trade, in particular on the import side, where the natural trading partners are developed countries (Ibid.: Table 4–6). The orientation of South Africa's trade towards these countries will be further strengthened in the future, due to the country's free trade agreement with the EU in 1999.

Macroeconomic Policy and Convergence in SADC FTA

International experience suggests that the promotion of growth through trade liberalization and regional integration has to be combined with policies aimed at macroeconomic stability. Besides, in order to achieve investor confidence it is of prime importance that macroeconomic policy is credible and sustainable (Gros and Thygesen, 1998: 480–85, Jenkins, Leape and Thomas, 2000). In developing countries, trade policy reversals are likely responses to current account deficits created by lax fiscal policies and overvalued exchange rates. Keeping budget deficits small helps to control inflation and avoid balance of payments problems, and maintaining a realistic exchange rate pays off in greater international competitiveness. Thus, the benefits of a free trade area will be much higher, and the collapse of the arrangement is less likely, if exchange rates are compatible with current account balance.

In an integrated area, it is highly desirable that bilateral exchange rates are consistent with two-way, balanced intra-regional trade. This results in benefits for all countries through expanding manufacturing production and non-traditional exports. In the SADC FTA this means increased access and increased exports to the South African market. In most of the SADC countries, however, diversification of the export base and a shift towards non-traditional exports requires new investments, and in order to attract domestic and foreign investments the region needs a credible institutional structure and a stable macroeconomic environment. Investor confidence may be in danger if large public sector deficits raise inflation and interest rates, crowding private investments out of access to domestic savings, and increase the risk of trade and macroeconomic policy reversals. This affects the international credibility, and growth and foreign investment suffer as a consequence (Fisher et al., 1998: 13, Jordaan, 2001: 86–87).

Country profiles and macroeconomic convergence in the 1990s

Over the last two decades, all SADC FTA countries have implemented stabilization and structural adjustment programs, either with the support of the IMF and the World Bank (Botswana, Lesotho, Malawi, Mauritius, Mozambique, Tanzania, Zambia and Zimbabwe) or on their own initiative (Namibia, South Africa and Swaziland) (Mistry, 1996: 167–69). The programs supported by the IMF and the World Bank contain two categories of policies: stabilization measures to restore macroeconomic balance, primarily by reducing fiscal and current account deficits, and structural adjustments to create conditions conducive to sustainable macroeconomic stability (Smith and Spooner, 1992: 61–64). The stabilization measures usually include devaluation of the currency for external balance and tight monetary control, and structural reforms invariably involve liberalization of trade and exchange rate regimes.

The large differences in economic structure mean that there are no a priori expectations of convergence among the SADC FTA countries (Jenkins and Thomas, 1998: 155–57). The dominance of South Africa in the region means that the growth and the adjustment process of that country will have major repercussions not only for its neighbours in SACU but also for the other SADC FTA countries. In South Africa, a major recession during the early 1990s led to stagnation of GDP and increasing unemployment (ILO, 1999: ii). Since 1994, GDP growth has picked up to a modest annual average of 2.3%, while the situation in the labor market has deteriorated further. Consequently, unless the growth rate increases significantly, South Africa cannot be expected to be a driving force in the region, or to support increasing imports from other SADC FTA member countries through such measures as asymmetric liberalization within the agreement. The deterioration of the economy led to a worsening fiscal position, but the potentially inflationary effects were controlled by very tight monetary policy. Since the mid-1990s the budget deficit has been reduced and inflation has been brought down, due to the strong commitment of the South African Reserve Bank to contain price increases. Between 1990 and 1999 the current account balance has, on average, been balanced with small yearly fluctuations.

Lesotho, Namibia and Swaziland have issued their own currencies, pegged on a one-to-one basis to the South African rand, and the CMA agreement provides for the circulation of the rand throughout the entire area. In 1976, Botswana chose to leave the common currency arrangement, but the country has consistently maintained a near-constant real exchange rate against the rand. The BLNS countries are also members of SACU, which is dominated by the largest economy in the SADC area. According to the SACU agreement, South Africa decides customs and excise policy and duty rates. These memberships impose constraints on the pursuit of an independent monetary policy and partly on fiscal policy as well. Consequently, monetary policy is tight, and the trade and foreign exchange rate systems are being liberalized. The close market integration means that the exchange rates of the BLNS country's currencies vis-à-vis the US dollar, commodity prices and thus inflation rate are closely tied to those of South Africa. The budget balance reported in Table 4 includes grants from foreign donors. In the same way as government revenue these grants make it possible to reduce the inflationary impact of government spending. In comparison to most non-SACU countries, the fiscal position of the BLNS countries is favourable, except in the case of Namibia, and so is their current account position, except for Lesotho.

Table 4. Key Macroeconomic Indicators 1990–1999

	Percentage of GDP (annual average)			Total external debt 1999 as % of GDP	Annual average net ODA[a] as % of imports	Average annual % growth	
	Budget balance[a]	Current account	NET ODA[a] (all donors)			Consumer prices	Exchange rates[c]
SA	-5.5	0.0	0.2	19.0	1.5	10.0	10.0
Other SACU							
BWA	4.6	6.2	2.6	10.8	6.1	11.0	10.7
LSO	1.8	-37.0[b]	17.2	81.5	10.9	11.0	10.0
NAM	-4.3	3.6	5.5	5.8	8.6	10.2	10.0
SWZ	-1.5	3.0	4.7	35.7	4.5	9.9	10.0
Non-SACU SADC FTA							
MWI	-7.8	-14.4	26.7	143.3	65.6	30.6	36.2
MRT	-3.5	-1.9	1.3	56.4	1.7	7.0	6.0
MOZ	-3.3	-29.1	46.8	152.6	96.1	35.8	33.8
TZA	0.6	-18.2	21.0	72.9	50.8	24.5	16.1
ZMB	-4.0	-15.0	26.8	213.2	62.9	70.6	62.5
ZWE	-6.8	-5.3	6.4	81.4	16.0	26.4	35.8

[a] The budget balance includes grants, while net official development assistance (ODA) includes both grants (inflows of unrequited transfers from official sources) for current and capital expenditure and disbursements of concessional loans.

[b] The major part of Lesotho's current account deficit is due to large imports related to the water transfer component of the Lesotho Highlands Water Project, financed by South Africa. From 1990 to 1999, 81.5 per cent of the current account deficit was covered by a financial inflow from South Africa, recorded in the capital and financial balance of Lesotho's balance of payment (estimates from Central Bank of Lesotho, 2001: 50).

[c] Units of local currency per US$.

Sources: World Bank, 2001b. Table 2.15, 3.3, 5.8, 6.22, 7.1, 12.1, 12.9; International Financial Statistics Yearbook, 2001.

The economy of Mauritius has performed well, and all indicators suggest that the macroeconomic policy adopted is consistent and sustainable. The basic aim of monetary policy is to achieve price stability and a stable nominal exchange rate, and the entire policy is supportive of increasing external trade. With the exception of a few years in the mid-1990s the budget deficit has been low and stable. From 1970 to 1997, Mauritius and the three SACU members Botswana, Lesotho and Swaziland were the four countries with the highest growth rates south of the Sahara (Petersson, 2001: 250).

The other non-SACU countries, however, are characterized by high and fluctuating inflation rates and large current account deficits that resulted in large external debts in relation to GDP in 1999. The nominal exchange rates in US dollars per unit of local currency have declined significantly, and the countries are dependent on large net inflows of grants, included in the budget balance. These grants have substantially reduced the budget deficits of most of the non-SACU countries. In addition, most of the countries have received substantial official development assistance in the form of concessional financial flows that aim to promote economic development and welfare. Since 1999 Zimbabwe has experienced acute economic difficulties: high inflation, high budget deficits, a rising domestic public debt, declining export earnings and declining outputs in key sectors such as manufacturing and mining. (Sadcbankers, 2001).

A main objective of all structural adjustment programs has been to bring large budget deficits under control in order to restore internal balance and debt sustainability. The focus has been on reduction of domestic expenditure, in particular current government expenditure, and on revision of the structure of taxes. The improvements in fiscal performance have been mixed, but for most countries budget deficits, including grants, have been reduced and stabilized at a lower proportion of GDP than in the 1980s. As seen in Table 5, the standard deviations for the budget balance from 1990 to 1999 have ranged from 1.4 to 3.1 for all countries but Botswana and Malawi (both 5.2).

However, a main explanation for the more stable and relatively lower budget deficits, as compared to the 1980s, is that increased grants constitute an important part of the structural adjustment package. Thus, if net capital grants are excluded, the budget deficits of Lesotho, Malawi, Mozambique, Tanzania and Zambia amounted to between 15 and 37% of GDP during the 1990s (World Bank, 2001b: Table 7.2). Consequently, macroeconomic stability is heavily dependent on the ability to sustain the current level of donor support. It appears that the positions of Mauritius and the SACU countries are much better than those of the other nations. The SACU experience suggests that a SADC free trade area would benefit from a credible collective agency of restraint, where the loss of access to the South African market would be an effective sanction.

Terms of trade development and exchange rate policy

Most SADC countries are primary exporters. Some export minerals, while others rely on agricultural or fishery products to generate foreign exchange. In several countries exports are highly concentrated to one or two products: diamonds in Botswana, tobacco in Malawi, prawns in Mozambique, diamonds and fish in Namibia, coffee and cotton in Tanzania and copper and cobalt in Zambia. According to Collier and Gunning (1999), the concentration of Africa's exports to commodities with volatile and declining prices has contributed to the slowdown of growth in the continent. All the SADC countries above with a concentration of exports to primary goods have experienced a deterioration in their terms of trade with quite large standard deviations in the annual changes during the 1990s (see Table 5). These swings contribute to the macroeconomic divergence, and the countries may have to respond asymmetrically to external price shocks.

Table 5 presents an indicator of whether terms of trade shocks hit pairs of countries symmetrically or asymmetrically (Aoki, 1981). First, for each year from 1990 to 1999 for each pair of countries, the sums of the changes in their terms of trade are calculated. As an example, between 1990 and 1991, the change in the terms of trade for Namibia was -18.3%, and for Zambia -26.4%. The sum of these changes is -44.7. The same calculation is performed for all years in the 1990s. The standard deviation of these combined yearly changes is calculated for each pair of countries.

High values indicate symmetrical shocks. Thereafter, the difference between the yearly changes is calculated (8.1 in our example), and the standard deviation of all years in the 1990s is calculated, representing asymmetric shocks. The indicator used in Table 5 is the ratio between these two standard deviations for each pair of countries. High figures (>1) indicate that symmetric shocks dominate, while small figures (<1) indicate dominance of asymmetric shocks. Values around 1 mean that no common trend exists. We have highlighted high figures of symmetric shocks between pairs of countries in bold (>1.25) and the most asymmetric pairs in bold italics (<0.75). Countries with a high export concentration in primary commodities are highlighted in italics.

Table 5. Indicators of Symmetric and Asymmetric Shocks to Terms of Trade between Pairs of SADC Countries, and Standard Deviations of Terms of Trade, Budget Balance and Real Discount Rate, Annual Changes 1990–1999.

	BWA	LSO	MWI	MRT	MOZ	NAM	SA	SWZ	TZA	ZMB	ZWE
Botswana	0.00	1.22	0.88	0.97	*0.74*	**1.34**	1.13	1.02	**1.34**	**1.27**	*0.74*
Lesotho		0.00	*0.61*	1.01	*0.75*	**1.72**	0.95	1.09	*0.75*	1.17	0.95
Malawi			0.00	1.12	**2.10**	*0.62*	0.98	**1.30**	1.24	1.00	0.97
Mauritius				0.00	1.08	1.02	*0.72*	0.91	0.93	1.00	**1.66**
Mozambique					0.00	*0.67*	0.91	**1.32**	*0.72*	1.00	1.02
Namibia						0.00	1.18	*0.54*	0.82	**1.44**	1.00
South Africa							0.00	0.92	1.17	1.05	**2.51**
Swaziland								0.00	0.97	0.86	0.91
Tanzania									0.00	**1.39**	0.92
Zambia										0.00	0.94
Zimbabwe											0.00
STANDARD DEVIATION											
Terms of trade	5.6	5.6	13.2	1.9	13.6	8.9	1.5	10.7	11.1	19.3	1.3
Budget balance	5.2	3.1	5.2	1.9	1.4	n.a.	1.7	2.8	2.2	2.8	2.2
Real discount rate	2.2	3.8	10.4	4.0	n.a.	3.5	3.3	4.1	13.0	21.2	6.3

Source: World Bank, 2001b, Table 4.7, 5.17 and 7.1.

The main point to be made from the table is that of 55 distinct pairs, only 11 indicate symmetric terms of trade shocks (>1.25), for the most part among primary exporting countries and among countries with relatively developed manufacturing sectors. However, a similar pattern is not found for asymmetric terms of trade shocks, and in more than half of all the observations there is no common trend of changes in the terms of trade between pairs of countries. Furthermore, the standard deviation of terms of trade changes is large for most countries with exports concentrated to one or a few primary commodities (see Table 5). Consequently, with respect to terms of trade development, the SADC FTA cannot be regarded as a homogeneous economic region. The explanation is found in large differences in the export structure between countries and in the price developments of different primary goods and between primary and manufactured goods. This has major impacts on the exchange rate policy, which is of crucial importance for supporting trade liberalization initiatives.

We have found that during the last decade or so, SADC countries have made significant progress with respect to trade liberalization and removed almost all restrictions on current account transactions. This has been accompanied by currency depreciation to support domestic producers facing increased international competition and to reduce initial balance of payments impacts of liberalization. The exchange rate policy is, however, complicated because the SADC countries face competing priorities for the exchange rate policy, such as stability of export earnings (in foreign and/or domestic currency), competitiveness, stability of import prices or minimization of the cost of the foreign debt service (Jenkins and Thomas, 2000: 49). The policy also has a regional dimension. The main share of primary commodity exports goes to the world market, but the main objective of regional integration and of the general push in the region towards increased trade liberalization is to develop non-traditional exports. This means expanding exports of manufactured goods, by improved access to regional markets – in particular the South African market – as a stepping stone to the world market. Consequently, manufactures must be competitive with South African goods. Thus, in Figures 1 and 2 we report real exchange rates in US dollars (an important currency for export transactions) and rand (an important currency for import transactions) per unit of local currency. The real exchange rate is expressed as the price in 1990 US dollars and rand, respectively, for a unit of 1990 domestic currency, based on official nominal exchange rates and consumer price indices of individual countries compared to the United States and South Africa, respectively.

The real exchange rates during the 1990s display large fluctuations, but at the end of the decade, as compared to 1990, all currencies show a real depreciation against the US dollar, except in the case of Tanzania. In that country, large inflows of development grants and loans may have supported a real appreciation between 1995 and 1998. On the other hand, since the mid-1990s, the exchange rate policy has not been uniformly supportive of regional trade liberalization aimed at increased exports to the South African (SACU) market. The South African rand has depreciated at a faster rate than other regional currencies (except those of Zambia and Zimbabwe) against the US dollar. The result is an increasing spread in the regional real exchange rates against the rand. Since 1995, all currencies except the Zimbabwean dollar have appreciated in real terms against the rand, reducing the competitiveness in the South African market. The conclusion is that although all currencies but that of Tanzania have experienced a real depreciation in their current main export markets (represented by the US dollar), since the mid-1990s, all currencies but that of Zimbabwe have experienced a real appreciation in the largest regional market, supposed to be the training ground for non-traditional exports.

Figure 1. Real Exchange Rates for Non-CMA SADC Countries and South Africa:
US$ per Unit of Local Currency

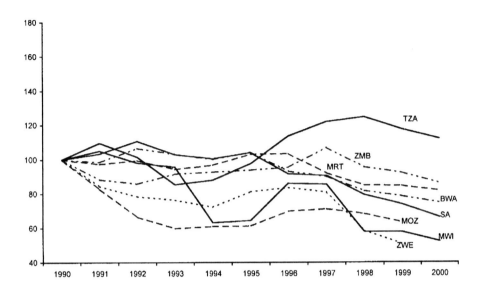

Figure 2. Real Exchange Rates for Non-CMA SADC Countries:
Rand per Unit of Local Currency

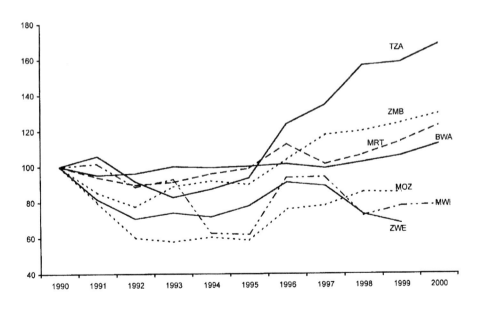

Source: International Financial Statistics Yearbook 2001.

Conclusions

In the course of globalization, trade within the major regions of the world has shown a stronger growth pattern than world trade as a whole. Thus, given the dominant role played by international trade in economic growth, the issue of regional economic integration becomes critical. In southern Africa, despite failure in the past, more rather than less integration is advocated, including investment cooperation and creation of conditions that will lead to convergence of the region's macroeconomic policies. The main objective of integration is to promote growth, and growth is usually seen as a result of the expansion of the industrial base. Macroeconomic stability is regarded as crucial for attracting investment and producing gains from regional free trade. The aim is to create a strong economic region, with increased interdependence between the member states, in a way that benefits all the countries of the region, and that eventually makes the participating countries competitive on the world market.

During the 1990s, non-tariff barriers were largely abolished and the spread of the prevailing tariffs across sectors and between countries was significantly reduced. Important steps were taken towards more uniform trade and exchange rate policies in an approach that built on open regionalism. However, few tariff rates were bound in the multilateral Uruguay Round, and there are large differences between bound and applied tariffs, which in turn leaves room for policy reversals. This reduces the credibility of the policy, because the experience of the past suggests that financial imbalances lead to reversals in the trade policy and exchange control reforms. Another weakness is the multiplicity of regional initiatives with a large number of overlapping and partially inconsistent arrangements.

The prospects of any free trade area are also reduced because of large differences in the economic structure and development of the countries in the region and by the asymmetry that is caused by South Africa's dominance. Mutual beneficial integration rests on the opportunity for the less developed participants to develop non-traditional exports, mainly manufactured goods, through access to the South African market. This scenario is not likely to materialize, however, due to the narrow export base of most countries in the region coupled with South Africa's growing import demand for differentiated products and its trade orientation towards industrialized countries. Another problem is that since the mid-1990s, all non-CMA currencies except the Zimbabwean dollar have appreciated in real terms against the rand, thereby reducing the competitiveness in the South African market.

Mauritius and the SACU countries have performed relatively well with respect to macroeconomic stability. The CMA has acted as an agency of restraint in monetary policy. The average annual rate of increase of consumer prices was low and stable during the 1990s, and only Lesotho displayed current account deficits. This stands in bright contrast to the situation in non-SACU countries that were building up external debts. In addition, for most members of the SADC Free Trade Area, macroeconomic stability is heavily dependent on donor support. A problem is that the countries whose exports are concentrated to a few primary products have large annual fluctuations in their terms of trade. Furthermore, the changes are not symmetric except for a few pairs of countries. The reason is found in large differences in trade structure among countries.

Although the integration initiatives, with the possible exception of SACU, have failed to achieve pre-established goals, the response to failure has been a demand for more, not less integration. The rationale of integrating small markets as a means to foster growth and development is clear, but the extreme differences among the SADC partners mean that the conditions (established by integration theory) for an equitable distribution of net gains do not exist. These differences are unlikely to disappear in the near future. However, cooperation and harmonization of macroeconomic policy and the gradual shift away from earlier import substitution policy, largely the results of structural adjustment programs, are steps that may facilitate regional integration as part of a general trend towards more liberal and export-oriented economies in the region.

References

Aoki, Masahiko (1981), *Dynamic Analysis of Open Economies.* New York: Academic Press.

Belli, Pedro, Michael Finger and Amparo Ballavian (1993), *South Africa. A Review of Trade Policies.* Washington DC.: Southern Africa Department, The World Bank.

Bhagwati, Jagdish (2001), *Free Trade Today.* Princeton: Princeton University Press.

BMR (Bureau of Market Research, University of South Africa) (1997), *The Southern African Development Community (SADC): A Socioeconomic Profile.* Research Report No. 244. Pretoria: Faculty of Economic Management Sciences, University of South Africa.

Central Bank of Lesotho (2001), *Central Bank of Lesotho, Annual Report 2000*, Maseru.

Collier, Paul and Jan W. Gunning (1999), "Why Has Africa Grown Slowly?", *Journal of Economic Perspectives*, 13 (3), pp. 3–21.

Fisher, Stanley, Ernesto Hernández-Catá and Moshin S. Khan (1998), "Africa: Is This the Turning Point?", *IMF Paper on Policy Analysis and Assessment (PPAA)*, PPAA/98/6, Washington DC.

Foroutan, Faezeh (1993), "Regional Integration in Sub-Saharan Africa: Past Experience and Future Prospects", in De Melo, Jaime and Arvind Panagariya (eds) *New Dimensions in Regional Integration.* New York: Cambridge University Press.

Gros, Daniel and Niels Thygesen (1998), *European Monetary Integration from the European Monetary System to Economic and Monetary Union.* New York: Addison Wesley Longman.

Harvey, Charles (1999), "Macroeconomic Policy and Trade Integration in Southern Africa". Botswana Institute for Development Policy Analysis (BIDPA), Working Paper No. 21. Gaborone: BIDPA.

Holden, Merle (1998), "Southern African Economic Integration", *The World Economy*, 21(1).

ILO (International Labour Office) (1999), *South Africa. Studies on the Social Dimension of Globalization.* Task Force on Country Studies on Globalization. Geneva: International Labour Office.

IMF (International Monetary Fund) (2000), *Trade and Trade Policies in Eastern and Southern Africa.* Occasional Paper 196. Washington D.C.: International Monetary Fund.

IMF (International Monetary Fund) (2001), *International Financial Statistics Yearbook 2001*. Washington D.C.: International Monetary Fund.

Jenkins, Carolyn, Jonathan Leape and Lynne Thomas, (2000), "Gaining from Trade in Southern Africa" in Jenkins et al. (eds) *Gaining from Trade in Southern Africa. Complementary Policies to Underpin the SADC Free Trade Area*. London: Macmillan.

Jenkins, Carolyn and Lynne Thomas, (1998), "Is Southern Africa Ready for Regional Monetary Integration?", in Petersson, Lennart (ed.) *Post-Apartheid Southern Africa. Economic challenges and policies for the future*. London: Routledge.

Jenkins, Carolyn and Lynne Thomas (2000), "The Macroeconomic Policy Framework", in Jenkins, Carolyn, Jonathan Leape and Lynne Thomas (eds), *Gaining from Trade in Southern Africa. Complementary Policies to Underpin the SADC Free Trade Area*. London: Macmillan.

Jordaan, André C (2001), "The Challenges of Globalisation for Development in Southern Africa", *Development Southern Africa*, 18(1).

Krugman, Paul (1991), *Geography and Trade*. Cambridge MA: MIT Press.

Lee, Margaret C. (2001), "SADC and the Creation of a Free Trade Area in Southern Africa", in Maloka, Eddy (ed.) *A United States of Africa?*. Pretoria: Africa Institute of South Africa.

Lipalile, Mufana (2001), "Globalisation, Regional Integration and Development in Southern Africa", in Maloka, Eddy (ed.) *A United States of Africa?*, Pretoria: Africa Institute of South Africa.

Lundahl, Mats and Lennart Petersson (1991), *The Dependent Economy. Lesotho and the Southern African Customs Union*. Boulder CO: Westview Press.

Maasdorp, Gavin (1998), "Trade Integration and Economic Development: Some Southern African Issues", in Lennart Petersson (ed.), *Post-Apartheid Southern Africa. Economic Challenges and Policies for the Future*. London: Routledge.

McCarthy, Colin (1996), "Regional Integration. Part of the Solution or Part of the Problem?", in Ellis, Stephen (ed.) *Africa Now. People, Policies & Institutions*. London: James Currey and Heinemann,

Mistry, Percy (1996), "Regional Dimension of Structural Adjustment in Southern Africa", in Teunissen, Jan Joost (ed.) *Regionalism and the Global Economy. The Case of Africa*. The Hague:Forum on Debt and Development (FODAD).

Ng, Francis and Alxander J. Yeats (2000), "On the Recent Trade Performance of Sub-Saharan African Countries: Cause for Hope or More of the Same?". Africa Region Working Papers Series, No. 7. Washington DC.: Trade Research Team of the World Bank.

Ottaviano, Gianmarco I. P. and Diego Puga (1998), "Agglomeration in the Global Economy: A Survey of the 'New Economic Geography'", *The World Economy*, 21(6).

Petersson, Lennart (2001), "Foreign ependency and High-Speed Growth in Lesotho", in Lundahl, Mats (ed) *From Crisis to Growth in Africa?*. London: Routledge.

Petersson, Lennart (2002), "Integration and Intra-Industry Trade Adjustment in South Africa", in *Development Southern Africa*, 19(2).

Robson, Peter (1997), "Integration in Sub-Saharan Africa", in El-Agraa, Ali M. (ed) *Economic Integration Worldwide*. London: Macmillan Press Ltd.

Robson, Peter (1998), *The Economics of International Integration*. Fourth Edition. London: Routledge.

SADC (Southern African Development Community) (1996), "Protocol on Trade", Maseru, August 1996. Gaborone: SADC.

Sadcbankers (2001), Recent Economic Developments for April 2001 (Zimbabwe), www.sadcbankers.org.

Smith, Lawrence D. Neil J. and Spooner (1992), "The Sequencing of Structural Adjustment Policy Instruments in the Agricultural Sector", in Milner, Chris and A.J. Rayner (eds), *Policy Adjustment in Africa*. London: Macmillan.

Söderbaum, Fredrik (1996), *Handbook of Regional Organizations in Africa*. Uppsala: The Nordic Africa Institute.

Svedberg, Peter (1993), "The Export Performance of Sub-Saharan Africa", in Frimpong-Ansah, Jonathan, S.M. Ravi Kanbur and Peter Svedberg (eds), *Trade and Development in Sub-Saharan Africa*. Manchester and New York: Manchester University Press.

Tsikata, Yvonne M. (1999), "Southern Africa: Trade Liberalization and Implications for a Free Trade Area", Trade and Industrial Policy Secretariat (TIPS) 1999 Annual Forum, 19–22 September 1999, Johannesburg.

Valentine, Nicole (1998), "The SADC's Revealed Comparative Advantage in Regional and International Trade", Development Policy Research Unit Working Paper Series 98/24. Cape Town: DPRU.

Venables, Anthony J. (1999), "Regional Integration Agreements: A Force for Convergence or Divergence". Mimeo, World Bank and the London School of Economics.

Viner, Jacob (1950), *The Customs Union Issue*. New York: Carnegie Endowment for International Peace.

World Economic Forum (2000), *Regional Economic Review: Southern Africa Summit 2000*, prepared by the SADC Finance & Investment Sector Co-ordination Unit (FISCU). Pretoria: Department of Finance.

World Bank (2001a), *World Development Indicators 2001*. Washington D.C.: The World Bank.

World Bank (2001b), *African Development Indicators 2001*. Washington D.C.: The World Bank.

WTO (World Trade Organization) (1998), *Annual Report 1998. International Trade Statistics*. Geneva: WTO.

6. Connecting and Disconnecting: The Impact of Globalization on Work in South and Southern Africa

Edward Webster

Work has always been a central social category in understanding society. Indeed, the birth of sociology as a discipline in the 19th century can be traced to attempts to understand the pathological and dislocating effects of the Industrial Revolution in Europe on the world of work.

Three phases in the social scientific study of work in South Africa can be identified:

— The first phase begins in the thirties when sociologists first attempted to understand the impact of rapid industrialization on the white community, and Afrikaners in particular. It was known at the time as the poor white problem. At the same time, but behind very different disciplinary boundaries, anthropologists were studying the impact of the migrant labour system on rural African society.

— The second phase begins after the Second World War when industrial psychologists – and later industrial sociologists and industrial anthropologists – embarked on microstudies of the workplace. The central concern of these social scientists was factors affecting productivity such as labour turnover, morale and monotony in industry. Some of these studies reproduced the notion that black workers were culturally different and, therefore, less productive. This could be described as a form of cultural racism.

— The third phase begins in the seventies when, under the impact of a surge of worker action and organization, South African sociologists fell under the spell of Braverman's classic study, *Labour and monopoly capitalism: The degradation of work in the twentieth century.* The rapid growth of labour process studies transformed the study of work in South Africa, leading to a range of studies on skill formation, racism in the workplace, Taylorism and Fordism (Webster, 1999).

With the opening of the South African economy in the nineties to international competition, the social scientific study of work was revitalised. We entered a new phase in the study of work where the world of work became a key national issue. The questions of international competitiveness, workplace equity and job creation became questions of national importance. Indeed, the Human Sciences Research Council (HSRC) set up a special fund dedicated to studies on People and Work.

From being an issue largely of concern to the academic world, the impact of globalization on the world of work is now one of the key issues facing policy makers in South and Southern Africa. It has also become a key research priority of the National Research Foundation (NRF).

Under the impact of globalization, South and Southern Africa are increasingly seen as part of an integrated regional political economy. I will, therefore, in this chapter, widen the focus of our concern with the impact of globalization on the world of work to Southern Africa as a whole.

Grounding Globalization

Anthony Giddens, in the 1999 BBC Reith Lectures, identified two broad responses to globalization – "the sceptics" and "the radicals" (Giddens, 1999).

The sceptics think nothing has changed much – it is all hype. "It is", in the words of Michael Burawoy summarising the sceptical position, "ideology rather than reality. The world is not that different today than earlier periods" (Burawoy, 2000:338). For many in the developing world, "globalization" is another manifestation of imperialism – the subordination of "the South" within the world capitalist system. In other words, there is no real need to think differently about the world of work in the era of globalization.

The second response is the mirror opposite –"the radicals" argue that everything has changed and see novelty everywhere. They, Burawoy argues, "believe that globalization is not just talk but refers to very real transformations that have dramatic consequences not only for the world economy but for the basic institutions of society – from sexuality to politics to the environment" (Burawoy, 2000:338).

Nowhere is this more evident than in the work of Manuel Castells, where globalization crystallises a new essence. For Castells we have indeed entered into a new phase of capitalist development (Castells, 1996). He calls this new phase of capitalism, informational capitalism:

> At the end of the twentieth century, we are living through one of these rare intervals in history. An interval characterised by the transformation of our "material culture" by the works of a new technological paradigm organised around new informational technologies. (Castells, 1996: 29.)

This has created what he calls the network society. For Castells the old was hierarchical, the new is based on networks. In his view, the network society results in labour becoming localised, disaggregated, fragmented, diversified and divided in its collective identity.

I am not persuaded by either approach: sceptic or radical. I would agree with Burawoy, when he argues that what is required is a "grounded globalization". Grounded globalization, he argues, is the antidote to the sceptics who ignore context and the radicals who have no sense of history (Burawoy, 2000:341–344). By grounding globalization we are able to identify the coexistence in Southern Africa of old forms of production – the extractive industries of the old mining companies such as Anglo American and De Beers – side by side with the new – the innovative retail sector companies such as Shoprite-Checkers.

What we see in Southern Africa, then, is a combination of "the radicals'" and "the sceptics'" view of globalization – a process of continuity of the past, a process "the radicals" ignore: with elements of the new, a process "the sceptics" deny. To understand this contradictory process of continuity and change, we need to ground globalization in the specific geographical and historical context of Southern Africa.

2. Grounding Globalization in Southern Africa

As Table 1 indicates, the Southern African Development Community (SADC) countries are amongst the poorest in the world, while the pandemic of AIDS is creating social breakdown on an unprecedented scale. According to the table, life expectancy is declining in the region and is likely, over the next decade, to decline even further. Some estimates of life expectancy are as low as 30 years by 2010 in certain SADC countries. Infant mortality rates and the Gini coefficients are amongst the highest in the world.

Table 1. Social and economic indicators: SADC region

Indicators	Botswana	Mozambique	Zambia	Zimbabwe	South Africa
Population	1.7 million (2000) est.	17 million (2000) est.	10 million (2000) est.	12.5 million (2000) est.	44 million (2000) est.
Economically active population (EAP)	850,000	8.5 million	5 million	6.2 million	17 million
Formal employment (% of EAP)	241,000 (28%)	750 000 (9%)	350 000 (7%)	1.3 million (20%)	7 million (41%)
GNP	US$4 922 million (1997)	US$1 700 million (1997)	US$3 600 million (1997)	US$8 600 million (1997)	US$130 000 million (1997)
GNP per capita	US$3 260 (1997)	US$80 (1997)	US$380 (1997)	US$750 (1997)	US$3 400 (1997)
Principal export	Diamonds (74%)	Shellfish (40%) and cashew nuts and cotton	Copper (52%) and cobalt (18%)	Tobacco (23%) and minerals and mineral products	Gold (21%) and other minerals and mineral products
Foreign debt	US$613(1996)	US$5 842 (1996)	US$7 113 (1996)	US$5 005 (1996)	US$34 540 1996
Life expectancy	47.4 years	42.2 years	40.1 years	44.1 years	54.7 years
Infant mortality rate	38 per 1 000	129 per 1 000	112 per 1 000	59 per 1 000	60 per 1 000
HDI	0.678 (1998)	0.281 (1998)	0.378 (1998)	0.507 (1998)	0.717 (1998)
Gini coefficient	0.54	Not available	0.50	0.63	0.59
Union density	16%	27%	30%	15%	57%

Source: SADC Regional Human Development Report 2000.

3. Legacy of White Settler Domination

Although the process of decolonization in the region began in the 1960s, the legacy of settler colonialism persists. It was only in 1994 that the last bastion of white political domination was removed with the triumph of democracy in South Africa. It was, in the words of veteran scholar activist, John Saul (1993), the end of a 30-year war in the region – a war fought by apartheid South Africa and Namibia, white Rhodesia and colonial Portugal, in defence of settler colonialism. The tragic results of this counter-revolutionary war can be seen in Mozambique today with 25 000 civilians disabled by exploding landmines. It can also be seen in the ongoing criminal violence fuelled by easy access to small arms.

The economic structure of the SADC region, according to the SADC Regional Human Development Report 1998, is founded upon the historical ambitions of white settler domination. This type of colonial structure, they argue, acts as a major constraint to the development of a diversified industrial economy in the region. The report identifies three constraints facing the region:

— *The persistence of extractive and export-oriented economies based on mining and agriculture.* The result is that transport networks were developed in order to open up regions where minerals had been discovered – such as the Zambian Copperbelt in 1920s – and to help transport these commodities to major ports for shipment to Europe.

— *Labour migration and its consequences* For over a century migrant workers from the SADC region were a source of cheap labour for mines, farms and industries in South Africa and Zimbabwe. Rural peasant families bore the main economic and social burden of the reproduction of the migrant labour force. Many of the social consequences of migrant labour, including the AIDS pandemic, originate in this disruption of families and communities in the rural areas.

— *Land dispossession and underdevelopment in the region* The unresolved land question remains a threat to political stability in a number of SADC countries. Land "invasions" in the white-owned commercial farming land by peasant squatters have already become a highly explosive issue in Zimbabwe (SARIPS, 1998:16–22).

I would identify an additional constraint arising from settler colonialism: the legacy of the apartheid workplace regime (Von Holdt, 2000). The apartheid workplace regime, Von Holdt argues, is the legacy of racism, low trust, low skills, high absenteeism, adversarial industrial relations, and a lack of identification by employees with the goals of the enterprise.

4. Implications of Globalization for the Region: A Process of "Connecting" and "Disconnecting"

There is a growing sense of desperation, even anger, with the effects of liberalization on the economy in the region. There is a lack of job-creating foreign direct investment. Indeed, one could argue that there is a process of "red-lining" of the region by the international financial community.

The marginalization of Africa is emerging as a key international issue: trade unions in the region reject the imposition of labour standards from the North. This is seen as a form of non-tariff protectionism and hypocritical. For example, the Organization for Economic Co-operation and Development (OECD) spends US$300 billion per annum on farm subsidies to member countries, equal to Africa's entire gross domestic product ("Help Africa Help Itself", *Financial Times*, 28 November 2000).

Policy makers are beginning to formulate demands that will strengthen Africa's voice in international financial institutions. This raises the broader question of the nature of the new international economic order and Southern Africa's location within it. What has the impact of globalization on the world of work been in Southern Africa?

All the economies in the region have been built around high protection barriers. The opening of these economies in the 1990s to international competition has had contradictory effects – it is leading to a process of "connection" and "disconnection".

5. Process of Connection

At one level it could be argued that the region is being drawn into the new global economy. The liberalization of economies in Southern Africa is having some positive effects:

— Firstly, under the impact of globalization, countries all over the world are forming regional trading blocs – the European Union (EU), the North American Free Trade Association (NAFTA) and Mercado Comum do Sul (Mercosul) in South America. The formation of SADC in 1992 is thus part of a global trend toward greater regional cooperation and integration.

— Secondly, globalization has accelerated communication within the region, and between the region and the world. At the centre of the new economy is information technology – cellphones, the internet, satellite television – opening up the possibility of instant communication on an unprecedented scale.

In 1994, for example, South Africa had four million fixed line telephones. By the end of 1999 there were more than 12 million telephones, of which more than seven million were cellular phones. This was the result of a vibrant cellular industry in the country, which has been responsible for a capital investment of more than 15 billion rands, the creation of some 60 000 jobs, accumulated turnover of 50 billion rands, a foreign investment component of more than 30 billion rands, and the expansion into six other African countries in six years (Knott-Craig, *Business Day*, 6 November 2000).

— Thirdly, globalization has widened consumer choice and introduced cheaper goods for the consumer. A clear example is Shoprite-Checkers, which has introduced "world class" shopping malls side by side with a much wider range of goods and services. Of course, this is a controversial point as many of the consumer goods coming into the region are illegal. In Maputo, the illegal importation of motorcar tyres is a serious threat to Mabor de Moçambique, a tyre manufacturer (interview with Director of Human Resources of Mabor de Moçambique, Dr Filomena Polana, 27 October 2000, Maputo). Management at the Mulungushi textile factory in Zambia argue that the selling of second-hand clothes from charitable groups in the North – what the locals call *salula* (to bend down) – is undermining the local textile industry. Above all, workers feel that they need protection against goods imported from countries that exploit workers, especially China where independent trade unions are not permitted.

— Fourthly, globalization has spread new democratic norms and notions of human rights. Zambia, Zimbabwe and Mozambique, for example, have benefited from the holding of multiparty elections over the past two years. As Hyslop argues, "globalization has been a democratising factor in Africa in that states practising human rights abuses have come under pressure from the international community" (Hyslop, 1999:9).

— Fifthly, globalization is encouraging the spread of new workplace norms. Through the International Labour Organization (ILO), collective bargaining is being actively promoted in the SADC region. Furthermore, the notion that there are certain core labour standards, considered to be fundamental human rights, is being promoted actively by governments, the non-governmental organizations (NGOs) and the international labour movement.

The clearest example of the positive effect of these new global workplace norms on employment conditions in the region is the case of the cut-flower industry in Zimbabwe (Davies, 2000). In order to market their flowers, producers have to meet high international standards regarding the quality of the flowers themselves, and the methods used to produce them. International labelling programmes governing waste management, occupational safety and employment conditions, and backed by NGOs in Switzerland, the Netherlands and Germany, have created a "market incentive" for farmers to meet environmental and ethical guidelines in their cut-flower production. Meeting these requirements has entailed higher worker training, which has in turn created job security and better working conditions for some workers, while decreasing the demand for seasonal workers.

— Lastly, liberalization of the economy has forced some companies to introduce modern human resource management and joint union management problem-solving mechanisms. Shoprite-Checkers is an example of a company in the region that has introduced sophisticated management-employee relations. The best examples of successful companies are drawn from South Africa where companies such as Daimler Chrysler in East London and Volkswagen in Uitenhage have introduced workplace innovation through collective bargaining.

6. Process of Disconnection

At the same time that some people in the region are being drawn into the global economy, a growing number are losing their jobs and joining the informal sector in a struggle to survive. It is leading, in the words of James Ferguson, to a process of "disconnection" (Ferguson, 1999).

Unlike delinking, Ferguson argues that disconnection is a relationship where one side hangs up on the other without necessarily cutting the links. For example, the liquidation of Zambian Airways in 1996 and the taking over of its flights to London by British Airways as its remaining "connection". He argues that globalization has come to mean a sense of disconnection. It is as if, as Owen Sichone (2000) argues, the region is being cast back to the second-class status from which independence had delivered it. This sense of going backwards, is what Burawoy calls "involution" in his research on northern Russia – a retreat of the majority of the population back to their own resources, intensifying household production and elevating women's previous role as organiser and executor of the domestic economy (Burawoy, 2000). Allast Mwanza, as illustrated in Table 2, describes a similar process in Zimbabwe and identifies the survival strategies of these vulnerable groups (Mwanza, 1999:52–54).

Liberalization of the economy has been accompanied by a shift towards neo-liberal economic and social policies such as the introduction of export-processing zones (EPZs) and privatization. It has also led to a drastic cutback in social services and support measures such as food subsidies. In Zimbabwe it led to food riots in October 2000.

"Economic reform" is not strengthening the newly established multiparty democracies. Citizens' lack of access to basic services makes a mockery of the idea of citizenship. Many argue that what is required is the notion of social citizenship, the right to income security and other forms of welfare such as education and health, a right to one's social heritage, and a right to live in a safe environment.

This is best measured through the concept of the human development index (HDI), introduced by the United Nations Development Programme (UNDP) in 1990. This measures the extent to which people can make choices in their lives. The HDI uses three criteria:

— Life expectancy

— Education

— Income

Table 2. Summary of survival strategies.

Area	Strategies employed	Remarks
Education	i) Sending secondary school children to live with the working spouse in urban centres where state-run schools tend to be cheaper.	Only open to those with working spouses. Accommodation constraints may also prevent use of this strategy.
	ii) Sourcing assistance from the Social Dimensions Fund.	This option is fast becoming unviable due to underfunding – sustainability doubtful.
	iii) Relying on networks.	More sustainable option even though not on formal basis.
	iv) Offering labour to school projects in lieu of cash for levies and building funds.	Has limited sustainability but potentially useful where applicable.
Food & nutrition	i) Altering consumption patterns by cutting number of meals per day.	This can be an enduring strategy if the meals are properly planned. Families are currently doing fine on two meals a day.
	ii) Eliminating certain food items.	Some modern foods can be replaced by cheaper but nutritious traditional foods. With proper education can be an alternative strategy.
	ii) Relying on kinship ties to ensure food sufficiency.	Can be strengthened if kinship ties are re-energised.
	iv) Working part time to raise money to buy food.	Only accessible to communities where part-time work is easily found.
	v) Barter trade.	This informal system has always worked, but is dependent on the availability of goods to barter.
Income generation	i) Relying on livestock sales.	Only open to those with livestock – such people are limited.
	ii) Sale of agricultural produce.	Not been a viable option in the past few years due to erratic rains and ESAP-induced reduction in acreage.
	iii) Diversifying sources of income, especially in microbusiness projects.	From the study, very little income appears to be derived from household business and other projects.
	iv) Self-employment.	In the current economic environment, starting self-employment activities has not been that easy.
Transportation	i) Cutting down on social travel and travelling only when it is essential.	Tends to isolate people and undermines social integration.
	ii) In rural areas people now walk more.	Not sustainable, especially as no community is self-sufficient and sometimes travel is necessary.

Source: Mwanza, 1999:52–54.

Democracy, it could be argued, cannot be consolidated without some notion of social citizenship. What is disturbing in many African countries is the growth of patronage politics and authoritarianism, which has been called the criminalization of the state. (Bayart, Ellis and Hibou, 1999).

In sum, globalization is leading to a contradictory process: a process of "connecting", which is drawing a limited number of people into a new regional elite. This elite is based on the foreign direct investment (FDI) coming into the region, predominantly from South Africa (47.4%) followed by the US and the UK (Kalenga, 2000). Much of the investment is a response to privatization. Essentially, this process is widening inequalities in the region. Already Namibia has a Gini coefficient of 7 and Zimbabwe one of 6.3 – figures that place these countries among the most unequal in the world.

At the same time as a few people are being drawn into this new economy, the majority are being excluded – they are being "disconnected". Is there a way of making globalization work for the majority of the people in the region?

Need for a New Approach to the Impact of Globalization on Work in Southern Africa

What are the implications of our findings for the changing nature of work in the region?

The establishment of SADC in 1992, and other forms of institutional co-operation such as SATUCC, have attempted to deal with the challenges raised by liberalization of the economy. The key question is how can labour shape the process of regional economic integration. There are two broad positions that are held: a "free market" position that involves deregulation and an acceptance of a "race to the bottom". This would inevitably involve a relaxing of labour standards and social policies to compete with other countries in the region for foreign investment.

In contrast, there are those who argue that regulatory policies and the harmonising of labour standards and social policy will assist countries in dealing with the negative aspects of globalization. In other words, a process of what could be described as, "levelling upwards". Is a process of levelling upwards feasible?

The key strategy currently being pursued by those, led by the ILO, who advocate levelling upwards is the promotion of collective bargaining in the region through reform of labour law. In furtherance of their commitment to collective bargaining, governments in the region have ratified the two most important core conventions on the subject:

— Convention 87 – freedom of association and the right to organise (Zimbabwe has not yet signed)

— Convention 98 – right to organise and collective bargaining

However, the limited capacity of unions makes it difficult for them to play an effective regulatory and collective bargaining role. This chapter suggests that the key resources for successful collective bargaining do not exist in the region. While the harmonization of labour standards is a necessary step in the direction of "levelling upwards", labour law reform *on its own* is likely to have limited impact as long as the social partners do not have the capacity to represent the interests of their constituencies. While labour law reform is necessary, what is also required is a reconceptualization of what is a radically different world of work. Increasingly formal sector workers and their trade unions only constitute a part—but a vital one—of a broad coalition of organizations and movements in the region.

The labour market in the region is being divided into two worlds— "the world of employment" and "the world of work". In the world of employment, work is seen as a commitment to the employee and enterprise, where the employee is given a degree of participation in decision-making and benefits. In the world of work, work is precarious, unsustainable and risky and social protection is non-existent. Instead of extending social rights to all citizens, the liberalization of the economies is transferring the responsibility for social protection to the households and to the poor.

This is leading to a social crisis where the very sustainability of communities is at risk. There is an urgent need for reliable social information on how rural households survive in situations of dire poverty. It has been argued that these households are more flexible as they do not rely solely on wages but obtain income from variety of sources including the informal market, subsistence, state transfers such as pension funds, and rent from lodgers (Smith and Wallerstein, 1992).

The spread of temporary insecure work, where only the minority of economically active population have a full-time job, has led the German sociologist Ulrich Beck, to argue that we are moving globally from a "work society" to a "risk society". He calls this the "Brazilianization of the west" and argues for the need to break the link between paid work and citizenship (Beck, 2000). He stresses the importance of what he calls, "civil labour", that is housework, family duties and voluntary work. He believes that this type of "work" needs to return to the centre of our attention. This can best be achieved, he argues, by developing an *active* civil society, which, he argues, is increasingly becoming a global society.

However, Ulrich Beck's argument presupposes that a reasonable level of employment and a comprehensive system of social security already exist. In the Southern African context this is no the case. What is required is a reconceptualization of the meaning of work in a context where the sustainability of the household itself is at risk. Instead of conceiving of commodity production as primary, Gabriele Dietrich turns our understanding of production and reproduction on its head, by arguing that it is the *production of life itself* that is "the basic production process", without which extended production is unthinkable (Dietrich 1996:344).

Above all, Beck's approach leads to a form of "left pessimism". It fails to recognise that globalization opens up opportunities as well as closing them down. In a nutshell, working people in the region are struggling for social inclusion in the world economy, not exclusion.

While it is premature to speak of the food riots in the region, for example, as forms of counter hegemonic globalization, the embryo of an alternative to neo-liberal globalization is emerging. To some extent it began, on a global scale, in Seattle in December 1999. Increasingly trade unions are working constructively with human rights and NGOs to counter the negative effects of globalization.

The Director General of the ILO, Juan Somavia, has called upon labour to be the core of a broad-ranging social alliance influencing the direction of globalization. (O'Brien 2000:552). His vision is of labour leading a "world social movement" to exert pressure upon governments to live up to the recommendations of the UN World Summit for Social Development held in Copenhagen in March 1995. He identifies labour as the key actor because of its long history of fighting oppression, existing organizational structure and greater degree of representativeness and democracy in comparison to many social movement actors.

To take advantage of the new opportunities opening up through globalization, labour will need to find a way of combining its involvement in international politics with the growing stress on bargaining at plant level. It will also need to recruit and develop new ways of representation appropriate to the new groups of flexi-workers emerging in the workplace.

As the ILO argues, this requires that:

— Trade unions consider developing a dual organising strategy including a "community based" approach to organising in conjunction with other "shopfloor" organising methods;

— Trade unions should establish mechanisms to systematically track contracting-out processes in order to identify potential members, specifically contract workers and home-workers;

— There is a need to build coalitions with appropriate informal sector unions and organizations that already exist. (ILO 2000:14)

This is a challenge that requires new knowledge, new concepts and new organising strategies. There are signs of such a new approach towards labour emerging internationally. In part this is a response to the end of the Cold War signalling the lessening of ideological conflict based on divisions over communism. It offers a radically new set of parameters for unions to organise across national divides that have formerly been forbidden territory.

— Firstly, the ICFTU is now recruiting leading union movements in the South. Furthermore, more and more multinational companies are being exposed to multinational bargaining pressures from a more internationally co-ordinated labour movement. Indeed, the widespread supply chains inherent in global production introduce new vulnerabilities in enterprises, exposing them to international campaigns (Ramsay and Bair, 1999). A clear example is the successful campaign conducted by ICEM against the international mining company, Rio Tinto (Lambert and Webster 2000). Codes of conduct are re-emerging as responses to these pressures. (Sable, O'Rourke, and Fung, 2000).

— Secondly, the technological revolution brought about by globalization can be used to activists' advantage – email, web-sites, databases and many other computer applications are being widely used around the world to find, store, analyse, and transmit information. The emergence of the Southern Initiative on Globalization and Trade Union Rights (SIGTUR), a network of trade unions from countries such as Korea, India, Indonesia, Brazil, Australia, and South Africa, is an example of the use that activists can make of the new informational technology.

— Thirdly, we see the emergence of global norms of workplace rights: the notion, that there are certain core-labour standards. Unions in the region remain at best sceptical of attempts to universalise labour standards. Indeed many see this as a non-tariff barrier: a form of protectionism. However to avoid a "race to the bottom", where mobile capital plays off workers against each other, certain unions are beginning to talk of the need for South and North to agree on a Global New Deal.

The terms of such a deal are yet to be debated but a clear basis for such an agreement would be an acceptance in the South of certain core-labour standards in return for greater access by developing countries to the markets and the capitals of the North. Such a "deal" would need to address the question of debt cancellation.

But to make such a deal possible, labour needs to overcome the growing representational gap, where the new world of work is eroding the base of unions.

At the core of this new approach to labour, is the need to construct a new political alliance or, what may be better described as, a social alliance. Constructing such an alliance is a political question and falls outside the scope of this report, but SATUCC, could through its regional links, play a valuable interlocutory role by helping ground such an alliance in the concrete conditions of working people in the region.

South Africa's growing involvement in the region has been described as a form of recolonization. There is a very real danger that the unrestricted play of market forces could lead to the re-emergence of an exploitative relationship of South Africa with the region. Indeed there is a danger that a form of "trade union imperialism" could emerge in which Cosatu defines its role in a narrowly national protectionist way promoting its own interests at the expense of the long-term interests of the region. As has been argued, "South African unions enjoy the advantage of numerical strength, financial self-sufficiency, research capacity and international stature. This enables Cosatu to be tempestuous and confident in labour issues, making them vulnerable to perceptions of arrogance, pride and trade union sub-imperialism, the 'Americans of Africa'" (Maserumule and Miller, 2000: 37).

There is, however, an alternative way of conceiving South Africa's role in the region: one that recognises its dominance but sees it as one in which it "acts in the long run interests of the region as a whole and guarantees the provision of collective goods, in a manner useful to all countries within the region and not only in the myopic national interest of South Africa itself" (Odén, 1997:26). Odén describes this as an example of "benign hegemony".

The question is whether a strategy of benign regionalism is possible. Odén identifies two necessary conditions for such a role.

> First, South Africa must have the capacity as well as the willingness to create and maintain a mutually beneficial hegemonic regime. Secondly, the other countries must be willing to let South Africa play the role of a benevolent hegemony, at the same time as they must have sufficient capacity to participate within such a regime (Odén, 1997:29–30).

Odén goes on to identify four dimensions of these two requirements:

— Political will,
— Economic capacity,
— Institutional capacity,
— Nation building and political stability.

This is the challenge facing policy-makers in South Africa and the region: to develop the political will to create a new relationship; to ensure that it is the state and not the market that is in the driver's seat; to develop the institutional capacity at national and regional levels so that agreements and commitments can be implemented; and to establish internal political stability and a minimum degree of political consensus across ethnic, political, and religious cleavages.

We believe that a strategy of benign hegemonic regionalization is possible in Southern Africa. However, currently the most dynamic regional force is South African capital. It is able to act faster, and tends to have short-term goals. But the concentration of workers in South Africa's multinationals opens up space for a form of counter-hegemonic regional identity (Maserumule and Miller 2000:38). It should also be added that the overall capacity of the states in the region to implement regionalism is weak.

At the centre of a new approach to development in the region is an emphasis on self-reliance. The apologists for an export-oriented model of development dismiss too easily internal demand. As is argued in the 1998 Human Development Report for Mozambique:

> It is not a matter of stimulating domestic demand artificially, but of investing massively so as to increase the production and, above all, the productivity of thousands of producers, as was

done in all Asian countries… (it would) be a process in which the African village is valued and becomes more productive: a process in which every year, out of millions of family producers, thousands become successful business people, assimilating new technologies, increasing their financial capacity, and creating new jobs. It means creating a national economy that is not so dependent on the outside, vulnerable to international shocks, a national economy in which increasing domestic demand is just as, or more, important than exports (UNDP, 1998: 86).

In a sense the majority of people in the region are being thrown back onto their own resources. This is the key to a more people centred developmental approach in the region. To develop such an approach the institutional capacity of the key actors in the labour relations system will need to be strengthened. By institutional capacity we mean the ability to implement agreements and commitments, to achieve compliance with partners and to adjust to changes in the local, regional and international environment. This requires a comprehensive human resource development strategy.

The changing global environment is posing a number of new challenges to the social scientific community in South and Southern Africa in the new millennium. How does one combine increasing productivity with employment creation? How does one provide for social protection in a market where a growing number of workers do not have fixed employment or a fixed salary? How do we regulate these forms of work? Can the state extend its protection to these workers? How would this be financed? Will the marketization, privatization and deregulation of the regional economy increase, or will there be a reaction against these developments? And if there is a reaction, what forms will it take? Will there be a return to economic protectionism or will new forms of governance emerge that can reduce the huge inequalities that have been expanded by neoliberal globalization?

These are the questions that need to be answered if Africa is to make its rightful contribution to global processes.

References

Bayart, J., S. Ellis and B. Hibou (1999), *African issue: The criminalization of the state in Africa*. Oxford: Indiana University Press.

Beck, U. (2000), *The Brave New World of Work*. Oxford: Blackwell.

Burawoy, M. (2000), *Global ethnography: Forces, connections, and imaginations in a postmodern world*. Berkeley: University of California Press.

Burawoy, M., P. Krotov and T. Lytkina (2000), "Involution and destitution: Russia's gendered transition to capitalism", *Ethnography*, 1 (1).

Castells, M. (1996), *The information age: Economy, society and culture, the rise of the network society*. Oxford: Blackwll.

Davies, R. (2000), *The impact of globalization on local communities: A case study of the cut-flower industry*. Geneva: International Labour Office.

Dietrich, G. (1996), "Alternative knowledge systems and women's empowerment: An organisational perspective", in N. Rao, L. Rurop, and R. Sudarshan (eds), *Sites of change: The structural context for empowering women in India*. New Delhi: FES and UNDP.

Ferguson, J. (1999), *Expectations of modernity: Myths and meanings of urban life in Zambia's Copperbelt*. Berkeley:University of California.

Giddens, A., (1999), "Run away world", *Reith Lectures*. London: British Broadcasting Co-operation.

Hyslop, J. (ed.) (1999), *African democracy*. Johannesburg: Wits University Press.

Kalenga, P. (2000), "Emerging trends and patterns of FDIs in Southern Africa", *SADC Industrial Development through Regional Co-operation and Integration Workshop*. Windhoek, Development Policy Research Unit, University of Cape Town

ILO, (2000), *Your Voice at Work: Global Report under the Follow-up to the ILO Declaration on Fundamental Principles and Rights at Work*. Geneva: International Labour Organization.

Lambert, R. and E. Webster (2000), "Social Emancipation and the New Labour Internationalism: A Southern Perspective", paper delivered at a conference on Reinventing Social Emancipation, Coimbra, Portugal 21–25 November 2000.

Knott-Craig, A. (2000), "Calling Africa – Is anyone home?" *Business Day*.

Maserumule, B. and D. Miller (2000), "Understanding regionalism in post-apartheid Southern Africa", *South African Labour Bulletin*, 24 (6).

Mwanza, A. (1999), *Social policy in an economy under stress: A case of Zimbabwe*. Harare: Southern Africa Regional Institute Policy.

O'Brien, R. (2000), "Workers and World Order: The tentative transformation of the international labour movement" in *Review of International Studies*, vol. 26.

Odén, B. (1997), "Is South African benign hegemony a condition for successful regionalisation in Southern Africa?" *African Journal of International Affairs and Development*, 2 (1).

Ramsay, H. and J. Bair (1999), "Working on the Chain Game: Global Production Networks and Their Implications for Organised Labour", paper to European Sociological Association, Conference on Will Europe Work? 18–21 August 1999.

Sable, C., D. O'Rourke and A. Fung (2000), "Ratcheting Labour Standards: Regulation for Continuous Improvement in the Global Workplace", conference on Citizenship in a Global Economy, University of Wisconsin, Madison. November 2000.

Saul, J. (1993), *Recolonization and resistance: Southern Africa in the 1990s*. New Jerwsey: Africa World Press.

Sichone, O. (2000), "A political economy perspective of the prospect of SADC", *SADC Industrial Development through Regional Co-operation and Integration Workshop*, Windhoek, Development Policy Research Unit, University of Cape Town.

Smith, J. and Wallerstein, I., 1992, *Creating and Transforming Households: The Contstraints of the World Economy*. Cambridge: Cambridge University Press.

Southern African Regional Institute for Policy Studies (SARIPS) (1998), "SADC Regional Human Development Report, 1998: Governance and human development in Southern Africa", *Southern African Political Economy Series Trust*. Harare.

United Nations Development Programme (UNDP) (1998), *National Human Development Report: Mozambique: Peace and Economic Growth: Opportunities for Human Development*. Maputo.

Von Holdt, K. (2000), "From resistance to reconstruction: A case study of trade unions in the workplace and the community, 1980–1996", unpublished Doctorate of Philosophy thesis, University of the Witwatersrand, Johannesburg.

Webster, E. (1999), "Race, labour process and transition: The sociology of work in South Africa", *Society in Transition*, 30 (1).

RESEARCH REPORTS PUBLISHED BY THE INSTITUTE

Recent issues in the series are available electronically for download free of charge
www.nai.uu.se

1. Meyer-Heiselberg, Richard, *Notes from Liberated African Department in the Archives at Fourah Bay College, Freetown, Sierra Leone.* 61 pp. 1967. (OUT-OF-PRINT)

2. Not published.

3. Carlsson, Gunnar, *Benthonic Fauna in African Watercourses with Special Reference to Black Fly Populations.* 13 pp. 1968. (OUT-OF-PRINT)

4. Eldblom, Lars, *Land Tenure—Social Organization and Structure.* 18 pp. 1969. (OUT-OF-PRINT)

5. Bjerén, Gunilla, *Makelle Elementary School Drop-Out. 1967.* 80 pp. 1969. (OUT-OF-PRINT)

6. Møberg, Jens Peter, *Report Concerning the Soil Profile Investigation and Collection of Soil Samples in the West Lake Region of Tanzania.* 44 pp. 1970. (OUT-OF-PRINT)

7. Selinus, Ruth, *The Traditional Foods of the Central Ethiopian Highlands.* 34 pp. 1971. (OUT-OF-PRINT)

8. Hägg, Ingemund, *Some State-Controlled Industrial Companies in Tanzania. A Case Study.* 18 pp. 1971. (OUT-OF-PRINT)

9. Bjerén, Gunilla, *Some Theoretical and Methodological Aspects of the Study of African Urbanization.* 38 pp. 1971. (OUT-OF-PRINT)

10. Linné, Olga, *An Evaluation of Kenya Science Teacher's College.* 67 pp. 1971. SEK 45,-

11. Nellis, John R., *Who Pays Tax in Kenya?* 22 pp. 1972. SEK 45,-

12. Bondestam, Lars, *Population Growth Control in Kenya.* 59 pp. 1972 (OUT OF PRINT)

13. Hall, Budd L., *Wakati Wa Furaha. An Evaluation of a Radio Study Group Campaign.* 47 pp. 1973. SEK 45,- (OUT-OF-PRINT)

14. Ståhl, Michael, *Contradictions in Agricultural Development. A Study of Three Minimum Package Projects in Southern Ethiopia.* 65 pp. 1973 (OUT-OF-PRINT)

15. Linné, Olga, *An Evaluation of Kenya Science Teachers College. Phase II 1970–71.* 91 pp. 1973 (OUT-OF-PRINT)

16. Lodhi, Abdulaziz Y., *The Institution of Slavery in Zanzibar and Pemba.* 40 pp. 1973. ISBN 91-7106-066-9 (OUT-OF-PRINT)

17. Lundqvist, Jan, *The Economic Structure of Morogoro Town. Some Sectoral and Regional Characteristics of a Medium-Sized African Town.* 70 pp. 1973. ISBN 91-7106-068-5 (OUT-OF-PRINT)

18. Bondestam, Lars, *Some Notes on African Statistics. Collection, Reliability and Interpretation.* 59 pp. 1973. ISBN 91-7106-069-4 (OUT-OF-PRINT)

19. Jensen, Peter Føge, *Soviet Research on Africa. With Special Reference to International Relations.* 68 pp. 1973. ISBN 91-7106-070-7 (OUT-OF-PRINT)

20. Sjöström, Rolf & Margareta, *YDLC—A Literacy Campaign in Ethiopia. An Introductory Study and a Plan for Further Research.* 72 pp. 1973. ISBN 91-7106-071-5 (OUT-OF-PRINT)

21. Ndongko, Wilfred A., *Regional Economic Planning in Cameroon.* 21 pp. 1974. SEK 45,-. ISBN 91-7106-073-1 (OUT-OF-PRINT)

22. Pipping-van Hulten, Ida, *An Episode of Colonial History: The German Press in Tanzania 1901–1914.* 47 pp. 1974. SEK 45,-. ISBN 91-7106-077-4 (OUT-OF-PRINT)

23. Magnusson, Åke, *Swedish Investments in South Africa.* 57 pp. 1974. SEK 45,-. ISBN 91-7106-078-2 (OUT-OF-PRINT)

24. Nellis, John R., *The Ethnic Composition of Leading Kenyan Government Positions.* 26 pp. 1974. SEK 45,-. ISBN 91-7106-079-0 (OUT-OF-PRINT)

25. Francke, Anita, *Kibaha Farmers' Training Centre. Impact Study 1965–1968.* 106 pp. 1974. SEK 45,-. ISBN 91-7106-081-2 (OUT-OF-PRINT)

26. Aasland, Tertit, *On the Move-to-the-Left in Uganda 1969–1971.* 71 pp. 1974. SEK 45,-. ISBN 91-7106-083-9 (OUT-OF-PRINT)

27. Kirk-Greene, Anthony H.M., *The Genesis of the Nigerian Civil War and the Theory of Fear.* 32 pp. 1975. SEK 45,-. ISBN 91-7106-085-5 (OUT-OF-PRINT)

28. Okereke, Okoro, *Agrarian Development Programmes of African Countries. A Reappraisal of Problems of Policy.* 20 pp. 1975. SEK 45,-. ISBN 91-7106-086-3 (OUT-OF-PRINT)

29. Kjekshus, Helge, *The Elected Elite. A Socio-Economic Profile of Candidates in Tanzania's Parliamentary Election, 1970.* 40 pp. 1975. SEK 45,-. ISBN 91-7106-087-1 (OUT-OF-PRINT)

30. Frantz, Charles, *Pastoral Societies, Stratification and National Integration in Africa.* 34 pp. 1975. ISBN 91-7106-088-X (OUT OF PRINT)

31. Esh, Tina & Illith Rosenblum, *Tourism in Developing Countries—Trick or Treat? A Report from the Gambia.* 80 pp. 1975. ISBN 91-7106-094-4 (OUT-OF-PRINT)

32. Clayton, Anthony, *The 1948 Zanzibar General Strike.* 66 pp. 1976. ISBN 91-7106-094-4 (OUT OF PRINT)

33. Pipping, Knut, *Land Holding in the Usangu Plain. A Survey of Two Villages in the Southern Highlands of Tanzania.* 122 pp. 1976. ISBN 91-7106-097-9 (OUT OF PRINT)

34. Lundström, Karl Johan, *North-Eastern Ethiopia: Society in Famine. A Study of Three Social Institutions in a Period of Severe Strain.* 80 pp. 1976. ISBN 91-7106-098-7 (OUT-OF-PRINT)

35. Magnusson, Åke, *The Voice of South Africa.* 55 pp. 1976. ISBN 91-7106-106-1 (OUT OF PRINT)

36. Ghai, Yash P., *Reflection on Law and Economic Integration in East Africa.* 41 pp. 1976. ISBN 91-7106-105-3 (OUT-OF-PRINT)

37. Carlsson, Jerker, *Transnational Companies in Liberia. The Role of Transnational Companies in the Economic Development of Liberia.* 51 pp. 1977. SEK 45,-. ISBN 91-7106-107-X (OUT-OF-PRINT)

38. Green, Reginald H., *Toward Socialism and Self Reliance. Tanzania's Striving for Sustained Transition Projected.* 57 pp. 1977.ISBN 91-7106-108-8 (OUT-OF-PRINT)

39. Sjöström, Rolf & Margareta, *Literacy Schools in a Rural Society. A Study of Yemissrach Dimts Literacy Campaign in Ethiopia.* 130 pp. 1977. ISBN 91-7106-109-6 (OUT-OF-PRINT)

40. Ståhl, Michael, *New Seeds in Old Soil. A Study of the Land Reform Process in Western Wollega, Ethiopia 1975–76.* 90 pp. 1977. SEK 45,-. ISBN 91-7106-112-6 (OUT-OF-PRINT)

41. Holmberg, Johan, *Grain Marketing and Land Reform in Ethiopia. An Analysis of the Marketing and Pricing of Food Grains in 1976 after the Land Reform.* 34 pp. 1977. ISBN 91-7106-113-4 (OUT-OF-PRINT)

42. Egerö, Bertil, *Mozambique and Angola: Reconstruction in the Social Sciences.* 78 pp. 1977. ISBN 91-7106-118-5 (OUT OF PRINT)

43. Hansen, H. B., *Ethnicity and Military Rule in Uganda.* 136 pp. 1977. ISBN 91-7106-118-5 (OUT-OF-PRINT)

44. Bhagavan, M.R., *Zambia: Impact of Industrial Strategy on Regional Imbalance and Social Inequality.* 76 pp. 1978. ISBN 91-7106-119-3 (OUT OF PRINT)

45. Aaby, Peter, *The State of Guinea-Bissau. African Socialism or Socialism in Africa?* 35 pp. 1978. ISBN 91-7106-133-9 (OUT-OF-PRINT)

46. Abdel-Rahim, Muddathir, *Changing Patterns of Civilian-Military Relations in the Sudan.* 32 pp. 1978. ISBN 91-7106-137-1 (OUT-OF-PRINT)

47. Jönsson, Lars, *La Révolution Agraire en Algérie. Historique, contenu et problèmes.* 84 pp. 1978. ISBN 91-7106-145-2 (OUT-OF-PRINT)

48. Bhagavan, M.R., *A Critique of "Appropriate" Technology for Underdeveloped Countries.* 56 pp. 1979. SEK 45,-. ISBN 91-7106-150-9 (OUT-OF-PRINT)

49. Bhagavan, M.R., *Inter-Relations Between Technological Choices and Industrial Strategies in Third World Countries.* 79 pp. 1979. SEK 45,-. ISBN 91-7106-151-7 (OUT-OF-PRINT)

50. Torp, Jens Erik, *Industrial Planning and Development in Mozambique. Some Preliminary Considerations.* 59 pp. 1979. ISBN 91-7106-153-3 (OUT-OF-PRINT)

51. Brandström, Per, Jan Hultin & Jan Lindström, *Aspects of Agro-Pastoralism in East Africa.* 60 pp. 1979. ISBN 91-7106-155-X (OUT OF PRINT)

52. Egerö, Bertil, *Colonization and Migration. A Summary of Border-Crossing Movements in Tanzania before 1967.* 45 pp. 1979. SEK 45,-. ISBN 91-7106-159-2 (OUT-OF-PRINT)

53. Simson, Howard, *Zimbabwe—A Country Study.* 138 pp. 1979. ISBN 91-7106-160-6 (OUT-OF-PRINT)

54. Beshir, Mohamed Omer, *Diversity Regionalism and National Unity.* 50 pp. 1979. ISBN 91-7106-166-5 (OUT-OF-PRINT)

55. Eriksen, Tore Linné, *Modern African History: Some Historiographical Observations.* 27 pp. 1979. ISBN 91-7106-167-3 (OUT OF PRINT)

56. Melander, Göran, *Refugees in Somalia.* 48 pp. 1980. SEK 45,-. ISBN 91-7106-169-X (OUT-OF-PRINT)

57. Bhagavan, M.R., *Angola: Prospects for Socialist Industrialisation.* 48 pp. 1980. ISBN 91-7106-175-4 (OUT OF PRINT)

58. Green, Reginald H., *From Südwestafrika to Namibia. The Political Economy of Transition.* 45 pp. 1981. SEK 45,-. ISBN 91-7106-188-6 (OUT-OF-PRINT)

59. Isaksen, Jan, *Macro-Economic Management and Bureaucracy: The Case of Botswana.* 53 pp. 1981. SEK 45,-. ISBN 91-7106-192-4 (OUT-OF-PRINT)

60. Odén, Bertil, *The Macroeconomic Position of Botswana.* 84 pp. 1981. SEK 45,-. ISBN 91-7106-193-2 (OUT-OF-PRINT)

61. Westerlund, David, *From Socialism to Islam? Notes on Islam as a Political Factor in Contemporary Africa.* 62 pp. 1982. SEK 45,-. ISBN 91-7106-203-3 (OUT-OF-PRINT)

62. Tostensen, Arne, *Dependence and Collective Self-Reliance in Southern Africa. The Case of the Southern African Development Coordination Conference (SADCC).* 170 pp. 1982. ISBN 91-7106-207-6 (OUT-OF-PRINT)

63. Rudebeck, Lars, *Problèmes de pouvoir pop ulaire et de développement. Transition difficile en Guinée-Bissau.* 73 pp. 1982. ISBN 91-7106-208-4 (OUT-OF-PRINT)

64. Nobel, Peter, *Refugee Law in the Sudan. With The Refugee Conventions and The Regulation of Asylum Act of 1974.* 56 pp. 1982. SEK 45,-. ISBN 91-7106-209-2 (OUT-OF-PRINT)

65. Sano, H-O, *The Political Economy of Food in Nigeria 1960–1982. A Discussion on Peasants, State, and World Economy.* 108 pp. 1983. ISBN 91-7106-210-6 (OUT-OF-PRINT)

66. Kjærby, Finn, *Problems and Contradictions in the Development of Ox-Cultivation in Tanzania.* 164 pp. 1983. SEK 60,-. ISBN 91-7106-211-4 (OUT-OF-PRINT)

67. Kibreab, Gaim, *Reflections on the African Refugee Problem: A Critical Analysis of Some Basic Assumptions.* 154 pp. 1983. ISBN 91-7106-212-2 (OUT-OF-PRINT)

68. Haarløv, Jens, *Labour Regulation and Black Workers' Struggles in South Africa.* 80 pp. 1983. SEK 20,-. ISBN 91-7106-213-0 (OUT-OF-PRINT)

69. Matshazi, Meshack Jongilanga & Christina Tillfors, *A Survey of Workers' Education Activities in Zimbabwe, 1980–1981.* 85 pp. 1983. SEK 45,-. ISBN 91-7106-217-3 (OUT-OF-PRINT)

70. Hedlund, Hans & Mats Lundahl, *Migration and Social Change in Rural Zambia.* 107 pp. 1983. SEK 50,-. ISBN 91-7106-220-3 (OUT-OF-PRINT)

71. Gasarasi, Charles P., *The Tripartite Approach to the Resettlement and Integration of Rural Refugees in Tanzania.* 76 pp. 1984. SEK 45,-. ISBN 91-7106-222-X (OUT-OF-PRINT)

72. Kameir, El-Wathig & I. Kursany, *Corruption as a "Fifth" Factor of Production in the Sudan.* 33 pp. 1985. SEK 45,-. ISBN 91-7106-223-8 (OUT-OF-PRINT)

73. Davies, Robert, *South African Strategy Towards Mozambique in the Post-Nkomati Period. A Critical Analysis of Effects and Implications.* 71 pp. 1985. SEK 45,-. ISBN 91-7106-238-6 (OUT-OF-PRINT)

74. Bhagavan, M.R. *The Energy Sector in SADCC Countries. Policies, Priorities and Options in the Context of the African Crisis.* 41 pp. 1985. SEK 45,-. ISBN 91-7106-240-8 (OUT-OF-PRINT)

75. Bhagavan, M.R. *Angola's Political Economy 1975–1985.* 89 pp. 1986. SEK 45,-. ISBN 91-7106-248-3 (OUT-OF-PRINT)

76. Östberg, Wilhelm, *The Kondoa Transformation. Coming to Grips with Soil Erosion in Central Tanzania.* 99 pp. 1986. ISBN 91-7106-251-3 (OUT OF PRINT)

77. Fadahunsi, Akin, *The Development Process and Technology. A Case for a Resources Based Development Strategy in Nigeria.* 41 pp. 1986. SEK 45,-. ISBN 91-7106-265-3 (OUT-OF-PRINT)

78. Suliman, Hassan Sayed, *The Nationalist Movements in the Maghrib. A Comparative Approach.* 87 pp. 1987. SEK 45,-. ISBN 91-7106-266-1 (OUT-OF-PRINT)

79. Saasa, Oliver S., *Zambia's Policies towards Foreign Investment. The Case of the Mining and Non-Mining Sectors.* 65 pp. 1987. SEK 45,-. ISBN 91-7106-271-8 (OUT-OF-PRINT)

80. Andræ, Gunilla & Björn Beckman, *Industry Goes Farming. The Nigerian Raw Material Crisis and the Case of Textiles and Cotton.* 68 pp. 1987. SEK 50,-. ISBN 91-7106-273-4 (OUT-OF-PRINT)

81. Lopes, Carlos & Lars Rudebeck, *The Socialist Ideal in Africa. A Debate.* 27 pp. 1988. SEK 45,-. ISBN 91-7106-280-7

82. Hermele, Kenneth, *Land Struggles and Social Differentiation in Southern Mozambique. A Case Study of Chokwe, Limpopo 1950–1987.* 64 pp. 1988. SEK 50,- ISBN 91-7106-282-3

83. Smith, Charles David, *Did Colonialism Capture the Peasantry? A Case Study of the Kagera District, Tanzania.* 34 pp. 1989. SEK 45,-. ISBN 91-7106-289-0

84. Hedlund, S. & M. Lundahl, *Ideology as a Determinant of Economic Systems: Nyerere and Ujamaa in Tanzania.* 54 pp. 1989. SEK 50,-. ISBN 91-7106-291-2 (OUT-OF-PRINT)

85. Lindskog, Per & Jan Lundqvist, *Why Poor Children Stay Sick. The Human Ecology of Child Health and Welfare in Rural Malawi.* 111 pp. 1989. SEK 60,-. ISBN 91-7106-284-X

86. Holmén, Hans, *State, Cooperatives and Development in Africa.* 87 pp. 1990. SEK 60,-. ISBN 91-7106-300-5

87. Zetterqvist, Jenny, *Refugees in Botswana in the Light of International Law.* 83 pp. 1990. SEK 60,-. ISBN 91-7106-304-8

88. Rwelamira, Medard, *Refugees in a Chess Game: Reflections on Botswana, Lesotho and Swaziland Refugee Policies.* 63 pp. 1990. SEK 60,-. ISBN 91-7106-306-4

89. Gefu, Jerome O., *Pastoralist Perspectives in Nigeria. The Fulbe of Udubo Grazing Reserve.* 106 pp. 1992. SEK 60,-. ISBN 91-7106-324-2

90. Heino, Timo-Erki, *Politics on Paper. Finland's South Africa Policy 1945–1991.* 121 pp. 1992. SEK 60,-. ISBN 91-7106-326-9

91. Eriksson, Gun, *Peasant Response to Price Incentives in Tanzania. A Theoretical and Empirical Investigation.* 84 pp. 1993. SEK 60,- . ISBN 91-7106-334-X

92. Chachage, C.S.L., M. Ericsson & P. Gibbon, *Mining and Structural Adjustment. Studies on Zimbabwe and Tanzania.* 107 pp. 1993. SEK 60,-. ISBN 91-7106-340-4

93. Neocosmos, Michael, *The Agrarian Question in Southern Africa and "Accumulation from Below". Economics and Politics in the Struggle for Demo-cracy.* 79 pp. 1993. SEK 60,-. ISBN 91-7106-342-0

94. Vaa, Mariken, *Towards More Appropriate Technologies? Experiences from the Water and Sanitation Sector.* 91 pp. 1993. SEK 60,-. ISBN 91-7106-343-9 (OUT-OF-PRINT)

95. Kanyinga, Karuti, A. Kiondo & P. Tidemand, *The New Local Level Politics in East Africa. Studies on Uganda, Tanzania and Kenya.* 119 pp. 1994. SEK 60,-. ISBN 91-7106-348-X (OUT-OF-PRINT)

96. Odén, Bertil, H. Melber, T. Sellström & C. Tapscott. *Namibia and External Resources. The Case of Swedish Development Assistance.* 122 pp. 1994. SEK 60,-. ISBN 91-7106-351-X

97. Moritz, Lena, *Trade and Industrial Policies in the New South Africa.* 61 pp. 1994. SEK 60,-. ISBN 91-7106-355-2

98. Osaghae, Eghosa E., *Structural Adjustment and Ethnicity in Nigeria.* 66 pp. 1995. SEK 60,-. ISBN 91-7106-373-0

99. Soiri, Iina, *The Radical Motherhood. Namibian Women's Independence Struggle.* 115 pp. 1996. SEK 60,-. ISBN 91-7106-380-3.

100. Rwebangira, Magdalena K., *The Legal Status of Women and Poverty in Tanzania.* 58 pp. 1996. SEK 60,-. ISBN 91-7106-391-9

101. Bijlmakers, Leon A., Mary T. Bassett & David M. Sanders, *Health and Structural Adjustment in Rural and Urban Zimbabwe.* 78 pp. 1996. SEK 60,-. ISBN 91-7106-393-5

102. Gibbon, Peter & Adebayo O. Olukoshi, *Structural Adjustment and Socio-Economic Change in Sub-Saharan Africa. Some Conceptual, Methodological and Research Issues.* 101 pp. 1996. SEK 80,-. ISBN 91-7106-397-8

103. Egwu, Samuel G., *Structural Adjustment, Agrarian Change and Rural Ethnicity in Nigeria.* 124 pp. 1998. SEK 80,-. ISBN 91-7106-426-5

104. Olukoshi, Adebayo O., *The Elusive Prince of Denmark. Structural Adjustment and the Crisis of Governance in Africa.* 59 pp. 1998. SEK 80,-. ISBN 91-7106-428-1

105. Bijlmakers, Leon A., Mary T. Bassett & David M. Sanders, *Socioeconomic Stress, Health and Child Nutritional Status in Zimbabwe at a Time of Economic Structural Adjustment. A Three Year Longitudinal Study.* 127 pp. 1998. SEK 80,-. ISBN 91-7106-434-6

106. Mupedziswa, Rodrick and Perpetua Gumbo, *Structural Adjustment and Women Informal Sector Traders in Harare, Zimbabwe.* 123 pp. 1998. SEK 80,-. ISBN 917106-435-4

107. Chiwele, D.K., P. Muyatwa-Sipula and H. Kalinda, *Private Sector Response to Agricultural Marketing Liberalisation in Zambia. A Case Study of Eastern Provice Maize Markets.* 90 pp. SEK 80,-. ISBN 91-7106-436-2

108. Amanor, K.S., *Global Restructuring and Land Rights in Ghana. Forest Food Chains, Timber and Rural Livelihoods.* 154 pp. 1999. SEK 80,-. ISBN 91-7106-437-0

109. Ongile, G.A., *Gender and Agricultural Supply Responses to Structural Adjustment Programmes. A Case Study of Smallholder Tea Producers in Kericho, Kenya.* 91 pp. 1999. SEK 80,- ISBN 91-7106-440-0

110. Sachikonye, Lloyd M., *Restructuring or De-Industrializing? Zimbabwe's Textile and Metal Industries under Structural Adjustment.* 107 pp. 1999. SEK 100,-. ISBN 91-7106-444-3

111. Gaidzanwa, Rudo, *Voting with their Feet. Migrant Zimbabwean Nurses and Doctors in the Era of Structural Adjustment.* 84 pp. 1999. SEK 100,-. ISBN 91-7106-445-1

112. Andersson, Per-Åke, Arne Bigsten and Håkan Persson, *Foreign Aid, Debt and Growth in Zambia.* 133 pp. 2000. SEK 100,-. ISBN 91-7106-462-1

113. Hashim, Yahaya and Kate Meagher, *Cross-Border Trade and the Parallel Currency Market —Trade and Finance in the Context of Structural Adjustment. A Case Study from Kano, Nigeria.* 118 pp. 1999. SEK 100,-. ISBN 91-7106-449-4

114. Schlyter, Ann, *Recycled Inequalitites. Youth and gender in George compound, Zambia,* 135 pp. 1999. SEK 100,-. ISBN 91-7106-455-9

115. Kanyinga, Karuti, *Re-Distribution from Above. The Politics of Land Rights and Squatting in Coastal Kenya.* 126 pp. 2000. SEK 100,-.ISBN 91-7106-464-8

116. Amanor, Kojo Sebastian, *Land, Labour and the Family in Southern Ghana. A Critique of Land Policy under Neo-Liberalisation.* 127 pp. 2001. SEK 100,-. ISBN 91-7106-468-0

117. Mupedziswa, Rodreck and Perpetua Gumbo, *Women Informal Traders in Harare and the Struggle for Survival in an Environment of Economic Reforms.* 118 pp. 2001. SEK 100,-. ISBN 91-7106-469-9

118. Bigsten, Arne and Steve Kayizzi-Mugerwa, *Is Uganda an Emerging Economy? A report for the OECD project "Emerging Africa".* 105 pp. 2001. SEK 100,-. ISBN 91-7106-470-2

119. Obi, Cyril I., *The Changing Forms of Identity Politics in Nigeria under Economic Adjustment. The Case of the Oil Minorities Movement of the Niger Delta.* 125 pp. 2001. SEK 100,-. ISBN 91-7106-471-0

120. Bigsten, Arne and Anders Danielson, *Tanzania: Is the Ugly Duckling Finally Growing Up?* 113 pp. 2001. SEK 100,-. ISBN91-7106-474-5

121. Chitando, Ezra, *Singing Culture. A Study of Gospel Music in Zimbabwe.* 105 pp. 2002. SEK 100,-. ISBN 91-7106-494-X

122. Kamete, Amin Y., *Governing the Poor in Harare, Zimbabwe. Shifting Perceptions and Changing Responses.* 67 pp. 2002. SEK 100,-. ISBN 91-7106-503-2

123. Schlyter, Ann, *Multi-Habitation. Urban Housing and Everyday Life in Chitungwiza, Zimbabwe.* 77 pp. 2003. SEK 100,-. ISBN 91-7106-511-3

124. Mans, Minette, *Music as Instrument of Diversity and Unity. Notes on a Namibian Landscape.* 55 pp. 2003. SEK 100,-. ISBN 91-7106-510-5

125. Leith, J. Clark and Ludvig Söderling, *Ghana–Long Term Growth, Atrophy and Stunted Recovery.* 110 pp. 2003. SEK 100,-. ISBN 91-7106-514-8

126. Olukotun, Ayo, *Repressive State and Resurgent Media under Nigeria's Military Dictatorship, 1988–98.* 136 pp. 2004. SEK 100,-. ISBN 91-7106-524-5

127. Agbu, Osita, *Ethnic Militias and the Threat to Democracy in Post-Transition Nigeria.* 53 pp. 2004. SEK 100,-. ISBN 91-7106-525-3

128. Akindès, Francis, *The Roots of the Military-Political Crises in Côte d'Ivoire.* 46 pp. 2004. SEK 100,-. ISBN 91-7106-531-8.

129. Kelsall, Tim, *Contentious Politics, Local Governance and the Self. A Tanzanian Case Study.* 75 pp. 2004. SEK 100,-. ISBN 91-7106-533-4.

130. Lundahl, Mats (ed.), *Globalization and the Southern African Economies.* 128 pp. 2004. SEK 100,-. ISBN 91-7106-532-6.